LEVERAGING BENEFITS OF REGIONAL ECONOMIC INTEGRATION

THE LAO PEOPLE'S DEMOCRATIC REPUBLIC AND THE GREATER MEKONG SUBREGION

DECEMBER 2022

 Creative Commons Attribution 3.0 IGO license (CC BY 3.0 IGO)

© 2022 Asian Development Bank
6 ADB Avenue, Mandaluyong City, 1550 Metro Manila, Philippines
Tel +63 2 8632 4444; Fax +63 2 8636 2444
www.adb.org

Some rights reserved. Published in 2022.

ISBN 978-92-9269-924-6 (print); 978-92-9269-925-3 (electronic); 978-92-9269-926-0 (ebook)
Publication Stock No. TCS220557-2
DOI: http://dx.doi.org/10.22617/TCS220557-2

The views expressed in this publication are those of the authors and do not necessarily reflect the views and policies of the Asian Development Bank (ADB) or its Board of Governors or the governments they represent.

ADB does not guarantee the accuracy of the data included in this publication and accepts no responsibility for any consequence of their use. The mention of specific companies or products of manufacturers does not imply that they are endorsed or recommended by ADB in preference to others of a similar nature that are not mentioned.

By making any designation of or reference to a particular territory or geographic area, or by using the term "country" in this document, ADB does not intend to make any judgments as to the legal or other status of any territory or area.

This work is available under the Creative Commons Attribution 3.0 IGO license (CC BY 3.0 IGO) https://creativecommons.org/licenses/by/3.0/igo/. By using the content of this publication, you agree to be bound by the terms of this license. For attribution, translations, adaptations, and permissions, please read the provisions and terms of use at https://www.adb.org/terms-use#openaccess.

This CC license does not apply to non-ADB copyright materials in this publication. If the material is attributed to another source, please contact the copyright owner or publisher of that source for permission to reproduce it. ADB cannot be held liable for any claims that arise as a result of your use of the material.

Please contact pubsmarketing@adb.org if you have questions or comments with respect to content, or if you wish to obtain copyright permission for your intended use that does not fall within these terms, or for permission to use the ADB logo.

Corrigenda to ADB publications may be found at http://www.adb.org/publications/corrigenda.

Notes:
In this publication, "$" refers to United States dollars.
ADB recognizes "China" as the People's Republic of China.

All photos are by ADB.

Cover design by Mike Cortes.

CONTENTS

Tables, Figures, and Boxes	iv
Foreword	vi
Acknowledgments	vii
Author Profile	viii
Abbreviations	ix
Executive Summary	x
I. The Lao PDR and the Greater Mekong Subregion Economic Cooperation Program	1
II. Integration of the Lao PDR into the Greater Mekong Subregion and the Global Economy	5
III. The Export Structure of the Lao PDR with the Greater Mekong Subregion and the Rest of the World	7
IV. Structural Transformation: Diversification and Upgrading	12
V. Diversifying and Upgrading: Capabilities for New and More Complex Products	16
VI. Upgrading Paths: Agriculture	19
VII. Upgrading Paths: Services	22
VIII. Upgrading Paths: Regional Integration for Expanding Global Trade	25
IX. The Fourth Industrial Revolution: Implications for the Lao PDR and the Greater Mekong Subregion	29
X. The Role of Cities as Engines of Growth: Agglomeration Economies	31
XI. Connectivity to Enhance Trade and Integration in the Lao PDR and the Greater Mekong Subregion	39
XII. Recommendations	43

TABLES, FIGURES, AND BOXES

TABLES

1. Estimated Catch-Up Dates for the Lao PDR with Thailand and the United States under Growth Assumptions — 3
2. Unexploited Export Potential within the Greater Mekong Subregion — 11
3. Nighttime Lights Data for the Lao PDR, 2000 and 2016 — 33
4. Provincial Trade Facilitation Index, 2017 and 2019 — 37
5. Travel Time, Distance, and Average Speed to Vientiane from Districts in the Lao PDR — 40
6. Average Time Needed to Reach Vientiane from Greater Mekong Subregion Capitals — 40

FIGURES

1. Volume of Exports by Country of Destination, 2016–2020 — 6
2. Volume of Imports by Country of Origin, 2016–2020 — 6
3. Export Structure of the Lao PDR, 2016–2020 Average — 8
4. Changes in the Lao PDR's Export Shares between 1996–2000 and 2016–2020 — 9
5. Share of the Lao PDR's Exports to the Greater Mekong Subregion and Non-Greater Mekong Subregion Countries, 2016–2020 — 11
6. Export Shares and Complexity Relative to the Global Average — 14
7. Upgrading Triangle — 15
8. Short-Run Upgrading — 17
9. Agriculture Share of Employment, 2000–2020 — 20
10. Short-Run Upgrading Triangles in Agriculture — 20
11. Services Share of Gross Domestic Product, 2000–2020 — 23
12. Services Share of Employment, 2000–2020 — 23
13. Services Subsector Shares, 2000–2020 — 23
14. Services Share of Exports, 2000–2020 — 24
15. Global and Regional Value Chain Participation for the Lao PDR — 26
16. Import Structure of the Lao PDR, 2016–2020 — 27
17. Export Structure of the Lao PDR, 2016–2020 — 27
18. Participation and Positioning in Value Chains: Innovation, Upstream, Midstream, Downstream, and Post-Production — 28
19. Urban–Rural Population, 2000–2020 — 32
20. Urbanization Growth Rates, 2000–2020 — 32
21. Why Agglomeration Economies for Productivity-Driven Growth? — 34
22. Policies to Support Agglomeration Economies — 35
23. Factors Perceived by Businesses to Significantly Impact Operations — 37
24. Logistics Performance Index 2018 for Greater Mekong Subregion Countries — 41

BOXES

1	The Greater Mekong Subregion Economic Cooperation Program Strategic Framework 2030	2
2	Clean Battery of Asia	9
3	Gender Equality and the Greater Mekong Subregion Economic Cooperation Program	13
4	Agriculture Development Is Essential for Structural Transformation and Inclusive Growth	21
5	Building Tourism Competitiveness	24
6	Greater Mekong Subregion Health Cooperation Strategy, 2019–2023	36
7	Landlocked to Land-Linked in the Lao PDR: 2010–2021 Achievements and 2030 Targets	42
8	Enhancing Collaboration in Trade and Investment under the Greater Mekong Subregion Program	44

FOREWORD

The Lao People's Democratic Republic (Lao PDR) is strategically located in the heart of the Greater Mekong Subregion (GMS), with its neighbors' major trade partners with the rest of the world. This represents an opportunity to leverage benefits from regional cooperation to escalate development progress. This is the premise of the GMS Economic Cooperation Program. Over 3 decades, countries in this region have worked together under this program to drive forward the goal of shared prosperity.[1]

The Asian Development Bank (ADB) has been a key partner in supporting development policy coordination among GMS countries through defining a practical, goal-oriented work program for promoting regional cooperation. Focus has been on enhancing connectivity, facilitating cross-border trade, and addressing shared regional concerns, such as the environment and health, among others.

This report builds on earlier work that helped to define the vision for the Greater Mekong Subregion Economic Cooperation Program Strategic Framework 2030 (GMS-2030) and beyond. It represents an effort to better understand how the Lao PDR may leverage benefits from regional cooperation and integration in driving forward its development agenda. It utilizes both new and traditional data sources to provide fresh insights that support program and strategy development to promote more inclusive and sustainable economic growth in the Lao PDR.

The report discusses the idea of using regional cooperation as a development escalator through three interconnected themes:

- Economic upgrading and diversification through integration with value chains
- Cities and their function as engines of growth through agglomeration of economies
- Connectivity infrastructure to enhance trade and regional integration

We hope the analysis from this report will generate dialogue and support the design of strategies and programs to stimulate more inclusive and sustainable economic growth in the Lao PDR and GMS more broadly. The Lao PDR and the Asian Development Bank look forward to continued partnership and collaboration toward this shared goal.

Phonevanh Outhavong
Deputy Minister
Ministry of Planning and Investment
Government of the Lao People's Democratic Republic

Ramesh Subramaniam
Director General
Southeast Asia Department
Asian Development Bank

---

[1] Members of the GMS are composed of Cambodia, the People's Republic of China (Guangxi Zhuang Autonomous Region and Yunnan Province), the Lao PDR, Myanmar, Thailand, and Viet Nam.

ACKNOWLEDGMENTS

This report was prepared by the Asian Development Bank (ADB) under the regional technical assistance project (RETA 9416) Sustaining the Gains of Regional Cooperation in the Greater Mekong Subregion. It draws from the March 2021 publication, *The Greater Mekong Subregion 2030 and Beyond: Integration, Upgrading, Cities, and Connectivity*, which was prepared by Jesus Felipe (team leader) in his role as advisor in ADB's Economic Research and Regional Cooperation Department (ERCD). This report was undertaken by the Lao People's Democratic Republic (Lao PDR) Resident Mission of ADB's Southeast Asia Department (SERD). The Lao PDR Resident Mission Country Director Sonomi Tanaka provided strategic guidance. The study was completed under the supervision of Senior Country Economists Emma Allen and Soulinthone Leuangkhamsing of the Lao PDR resident mission. Mai Lin Villaruel and Rene Cris Rivera of the Macroeconomic Research Division of the ERCD provided valuable technical support for the study. Eric Sidgwick and Rattanatay Luanglatbandith, senior consultants to the Lao PDR resident mission, provided reviews and critical guidance during the preparation of the report. Josef Yap provided economic editing of early versions of the report. Maylee Phommachanh and Kheuavanh Phanthaboun of the Lao PDR resident mission provided administrative support. Souphavanh Phonmany of the Lao PDR resident mission provided support for printing and publication request.

Under the guidance of Alfredo Perdiguero, Asadullah Sumbal, and Maria Josephine Duque-Comia of the Regional Cooperation and Operations Coordination Division of SERD at ADB provided technical assistance and implementation support. This study benefited from the invaluable comments of peer reviewers at ADB, including Pinsuda Alexander, Thuy Trang Dang, Daisuke Mizusawa, Kanya Satyani Sasradipoera, James Villafuerte, Omer Zafar, and Dulce Zara of SERD; Sanchita Basu Das of the Regional Cooperation and Integration Division of ERCD; and Nguyen Ba Hung and Akira Matsunaga of the Sustainable Development and Climate Change Department. ADB's Department of Communications provided final review and assistance in the printing and web publication of the report. This study is a product of consultations with key government ministries in the Lao PDR and their agencies. We are especially grateful to the Ministry of Planning and Investment for its support.

This study is a product of consultation with key government ministries in the Lao PDR and their agencies. We appreciate the support of the Department of International Cooperation and the Development Research Institute of the Ministry of Planning and Investment, including Sisomboun Ounavong, Vanpheng Sengmanothong, Chanthaly Chansompheng, Lattanakhone Outhaiyavong, Vilasack Xayaphet, Ampy Sybounhueang, and Bouphavanh Keomixay. In addition, we are grateful for the support from Vithavath Inthivong of the Ministry of Foreign Affairs, Khamsonvong Phutdavong of the Ministry of Industry and Commerce, Sakpasit Manibod of the Ministry of Agriculture and Forestry, and Chandaly Sitpraxay of the Ministry of Health.

AUTHOR PROFILE

Emma R. Allen is a senior country economist at the Lao People's Democratic Republic (Lao PDR) Resident Mission of the Asian Development Bank (ADB). Her current responsibilities include heading the economics, strategy, and programming unit of the resident mission. She prepares the Lao PDR chapter for ADB's flagship publication, *Asian Development Outlook*, as well as ADB's country programming and strategy documents for the Lao PDR. She also supports the design and implementation of ADB loans and technical assistance related to public financial management, reform of state-owned enterprises, Sustainable Development Goals, knowledge and analytical support, and business environment. Before joining ADB in 2016, she was a labor market economist with the International Labour Organization. She received her PhD in economics and her bachelor's degree in combined economics and education from the University of Newcastle, Australia, in 2015 and 2004, respectively.

Mai Lin Villaruel is an economics officer in the Macroeconomics Research Division of the Economic Research and Cooperation Department of ADB. She is part of the team that produces *Asian Development Outlook* and *Asia Bond Monitor*. She holds a master's degree in applied statistics from Macquarie University in Sydney, Australia.

Soulinthone Leuangkhamsing is a senior economics officer at the Lao PDR Resident Mission. Before joining ADB in 2008, he was an economist at the Lao PDR Resident Representative Office of the International Monetary Fund. He participated in the preparation of the *Asian Development Outlook*'s Lao chapter, annual country programming, and country partnership strategy. He also supported the processing and implementation of the governance and public finance management programs. He holds a master's degree in business administration from the School of Management of the Asian Institute of Technology in Thailand and a bachelor of economics from Flinders University in Adelaide, South Australia.

Rene Cris P. Rivera is a consultant working for the Macroeconomics Research Division of the Economic Research and Cooperation Department of ADB. He is part of the team that produces the *Asian Development Outlook*. He holds a master's degree in public policy from Hitotsubashi University in Tokyo, Japan.

ABBREVIATIONS

ADB	Asian Development Bank
ADO	Asian Development Outlook
COVID-19	coronavirus disease
ERCD	Economic Research and Regional Cooperation Department
GDP	gross domestic product
GMS	Greater Mekong Subregion
GMS-2030	Greater Mekong Subregion Economic Cooperation Program Strategic Framework 2030
GVC	global value chain
ILO	International Labour Organization
Lao PDR	Lao People's Democratic Republic
MW	megawatt
PRC	People's Republic of China
RCEP	Regional Comprehensive Economic Partnership
SERD	Southeast Asia Department
SEZ	special economic zone
SMEs	small and medium-sized enterprises
US	United States

EXECUTIVE SUMMARY

The Greater Mekong Subregion (GMS) Economic Cooperation Program provides a platform for regional cooperation and integration to accelerate development and promote inclusive and equitable growth. Accelerating growth requires upgrading existing production structures and trading positions, while also expanding into new products and services with new trading partners. The Lao People's Democratic Republic (Lao PDR), a member of the GMS, has a comparatively limited trade basket dominated by primary and low-technology sectors. It also relies heavily on the GMS for both exports and imports, with limited expansion in trade with other countries in the global economy.

Rationale: Regional Cooperation as a Development Escalator

Though a landlocked country, the Lao PDR is strategically located, and is neighbor to major global trading partners. The country's limited trading basket indicates that there may be unexploited potential for expanding into more diverse products that are traded with regional and global partners. A potential pathway for diversification is developing shared production and export capabilities through greater regional cooperation. Therefore, an important issue for national and regional policy is how to encourage the spread of capabilities, technology, knowledge, and network linkages between GMS neighboring countries to support per capita growth spillovers. The GMS Economic Cooperation Program Strategic Framework 2030 responds to this need by leveraging its strengths of "competitiveness," "community," and "connectivity" to promote convergence in income and in living standards between member countries. GMS members such as the Lao PDR will need to grow significantly faster than the more advanced members, so that convergence becomes a reality. Economic policies and interventions for boosting growth and driving the process of structural transformation are therefore critical.

Pathway I: Upgrading and Diversification through Integration with Value Chains

Economic upgrading involves building on existing production capabilities while investing in new capabilities to accelerate the process of structural transformation. Production capabilities are shared among products, and as comparative advantage is gained in new products, more opportunities to diversify become available. Currently, there are only a few sectors where the Lao PDR produces goods that have product complexity scores higher than the global average. Most of these are associated with primary and low-tech industries. Understanding these opportunities can help to create short-run export diversification opportunities for driving the process of structural transformation. Engaging in value chains can also open more opportunities for deepening integration in regional and global trade. The Lao PDR's participation in value chains has increased steadily, but most activities are positioned "upstream," as a provider of raw materials and primary products that support the production of goods for exporting activities in other GMS countries. "Upstream" positioning in value chains is associated with low wages, while "downstream" positioning is associated with higher wages. It is therefore important to deepen integration in value chains, particularly in "downstream" activities. Promoting cities and improving connectivity are an integral part of this.

Pathway II: Cities Function as Engines of Growth through Agglomeration of Economies

Urbanization plays a pivotal role in driving structural transformation, but for the Lao PDR, the link between urban expansion and the economy has been weak. This is likely due to urbanization driven by the emergence of many small cities, which has resulted in more limited clustering of productive industries and resources. In 2020, one-in-three people lived in urban areas, with urban dwellers expanding by a moderate 3.3% per annum over the last decade. By 2025, one-in-two people are expected to live in urban areas. Although urbanization has proceeded at a pace, the country's cities have remained relatively small. Only Vientiane has grown substantially, reaching 1.4 million people in 2020 according to estimates from nighttime lights data, with other cities in the Lao PDR having less than 300,000 inhabitants. In the absence of urban development that drives growth through agglomeration economies, the process of economic diversification for structural transformation may continue to lag. Agglomeration economies in cities drive productivity gains by improving the sharing and matching of resources, while also enabling greater interactions for learning and knowledge spillovers. Policies to support agglomeration economies in cities include investments in urban infrastructure, as well as policies that create a conducive environment for doing business.

Pathway III: Connectivity to Enhance Trade and Regional Integration

Connectivity in the Lao PDR is challenged due to its mountainous landscape and associated difficulties in building straight-line and shorter road routes. The average speed traveled in the Lao PDR is 50 kilometers per hour. Districts in the Lao PDR take an average of 9 hours to reach the Lao PDR capital Vientiane. However, districts in the Lao PDR take only 14 hours to reach Bangkok or 16 hours to reach Ha Noi, where the markets are larger. In this context, transport network investments to facilitate cross-border trade are needed to open access to larger markets. Many district arterial roads that provide connection to such markets need upgrading, rehabilitation, and/or maintenance. Much of the transport network comprises earthen roads or gravel roads that become impassable during the rainy season, thus increasing transportation costs. Connectivity investments in logistics performance are also needed, to ensure that cargo reaches its destination within an expected delivery schedule. Because of poor connectivity, some districts may lack access to competitive economic services and markets in Vientiane or other major urban centers in the Lao PDR. Thus, they focus their efforts on cross-border trade with larger markets. The government is taking proactive steps to address connectivity issues, including adopting a strategic plan to turn the country from landlocked to land-linked through developing corridors that connect the country with its neighbors. This includes investments in economic and multimodal transport infrastructure, energy connectivity, and trade and investment facilitation initiatives.

GMS Summit. The Lao PDR hosts the GMS Summit in 2008 in Vientiane.

I

THE LAO PDR AND THE GREATER MEKONG SUBREGION ECONOMIC COOPERATION PROGRAM

The Lao People's Democratic Republic (Lao PDR) has achieved impressive growth and development gains in the 3 decades leading up to 2022. Much of the country's development gains have relied on converting its natural resource wealth into exports, with flagship investments made in hydropower for supplying clean energy to its neighbors. Improvements in connectivity have contributed to better market access for agricultural produce and led to declines in poverty. However, the country's growth has lacked inclusivity and has not resulted in an upgrading and transformation of the economic structure that advances living standards to levels observed in other countries in the Greater Mekong Subregion (GMS).

The GMS is made up of Cambodia, the Lao PDR, Myanmar, Thailand, Viet Nam, and the People's Republic of China (PRC), specifically the Guangxi Zhuang Autonomous Region and Yunnan Province. Since 1992, these countries have worked through an economic cooperation program known as the "GMS Program," designed to use regional cooperation as a development escalator for those under its purview. The objective of the GMS Program is to help converge economic growth and living standards of its members. The program's key target is the decline of income disparity within and between countries. The GMS regional cooperation program intends to help its members grow in such a way that all GMS members' income per capita converges with those of the highest income members.

The program is flexible and has been augmented over time to respond to various emergencies, such as the COVID-19 pandemic, with specific plans designed to deal directly with the repercussions of these incidences by leveraging benefits of regional cooperation and integration to protect the most vulnerable and maintain open trade across countries. The most recent strategic framework of the program is presented in Box 1.

Box 1: The Greater Mekong Subregion Economic Cooperation Program Strategic Framework 2030

The Greater Mekong Subregion (GMS) Economic Cooperation Program Strategic Framework 2030 provides a setting for subregional development over the next decade. The program is based on deepening regional cooperation and integration. It is predicated on three pillars:

(i) to build a greater sense of "community" through environmental sustainability and "one health" approach,

(ii) to achieve increased "connectivity" in terms of transport and energy, and

(iii) to enhance "competitiveness" by promoting trade and investment.

The program's acknowledged strengths of community, connectivity, and competitiveness, are to be deployed to address seven mega-trends foreseen to impact on the region's development performance and prospects:

(i) risk of pandemics;

(ii) weaker global growth and the threat to free trade;

(iii) persistent pockets of poverty and increasing in-country inequality;

(iv) severe environmental challenges and threats from climate change, disaster events, and pollution;

(v) technological change and digitalization;

(vi) evolving demographics; and

(vii) rapid urbanization.

To bolster the region's resilience, the program will support innovative solutions including (i) digital integration, (ii) spatial approaches, (iii) deepening dialogue, knowledge and capacity, (iv) private sector solutions, (v) cooperation with other regional integration initiatives, and (vi) results-driven approach. In addition, the GMS-2030 program is supplemented by ADB's Greater Mekong Subregion COVID-19 Response and Recovery Plan for 2021–2023[a] with three pillars:

- Pillar 1 protects lives following a "one health" approach, which acknowledges interlinkages between the health of humans, animals, agriculture, and urban environments;
- Pillar 2 protects the vulnerable and poor by offering them opportunities in border areas and GMS economic corridors, as well as supporting the safe and orderly movement of labor;
- Pillar 3 ensures that borders remain open to support green and resilient economic activities, facilitate transport and trade, rebuild agriculture, and generate safe and seamless tourism opportunities.

[a] ADB. 2021. *Greater Mekong Subregion COVID-19 Response and Recovery Plan 2021–2023*. Manila.
Source: ADB. 2021. *The Greater Mekong Subregion Economic Cooperation Program Strategic Framework 2030*. Manila.

The GMS Program has made considerable progress in supporting its member countries achieve per capita income growth and lifting people out of poverty, but little progress has been made in terms of inter-country convergence across the GMS countries. At the inception of the GMS Program in 1992, per capita income differences among its members were large. Although the GMS members with the lowest gross domestic product (GDP) per capita have grown faster over the last 3 decades, this higher growth has not been adequate to catch up with other GMS countries that had significantly higher per capita income from the outset.[1] To illustrate, in 1992, the Lao PDR's current per capita income was $250. Despite economic growth averaging 7% over 3 decades, the Lao PDR's current per capita income reached only $2,630 in 2020. In comparison, Thailand's and the PRC's current per capita income was $1,928 and $366 in 1992 and rose to $7,189 and $10,434 in 2020, respectively.[2] To achieve the objective of convergence, higher economic growth is a necessary condition for the members of the subregion, particularly the Lao PDR, to advance. The persistent gap in incomes between countries means that the program needs to ensure that countries such as the Lao PDR grow significantly faster than the more advanced members, so that convergence becomes a reality.

A further aim of the regional cooperation program is to support convergence of the GMS members with the global economic frontier. Progress toward this objective has been weak. Table 1 shows a simulation to demonstrate why growth matters and why convergence is an important policy objective. The data shows that if the Lao PDR grew by a very high annual average of 8%, it would take only 15 years to reach Thailand's 2020 per capita income. In contrast, if annual average growth rates remain intermediate and in the range of 4%, it will take more than 25 years to catch up to Thailand's per capita income in 2020. To reach the same level of per capita income that the United States (US) had in 2020, it would require an annual average growth of 8% for more than 40 years. The rate of convergence for the Lao PDR would also depend on the growth performance in other GMS countries, especially in the PRC, Thailand, and Viet Nam. This highlights the need to focus on economic policies and interventions for boosting growth to advance and converge with living standards in other countries in the region and the rest of the world in the coming decades.

Table 1: Estimated Catch-Up Dates for the Lao PDR with Thailand and the United States under Growth Assumptions

Item	With Thailand's GDP Current US per Capita in 2020 ($7,189)	With the US GDP Current US per Capita in 2020 ($63,593)
Low growth (2% per annum)	2071	2181
Intermediate growth (4% per annum)	2046	2102
High growth (6% per annum)	2038	2075
Very high growth (8% per annum)	2034	2062

GDP = gross domestic product, Lao PDR = Lao People's Democratic Republic, US = United States.
Source: Authors' calculations based on current US per capita income of $2,630 in 2020 for the Lao PDR.

---

[1] ADB. 2021. *The Greater Mekong Subregion 2030 and Beyond: Integration, Upgrading, Cities, and Connectivity*. Manila.
[2] World Bank. 2021. *World Development Indicators*. Washington, DC.

Boosting a country's economic growth and living standards requires successful navigation of structural transformation and greater integration of the national economy with regional and global trade. The key question is how to diversify and what potential options could be leveraged to support an acceleration of this process. An option for the Lao PDR and other GMS members is to leverage the benefits of regional cooperation and integration to accelerate the process of upgrading and diversification.

This report draws from the March 2021 ADB publication, *The Greater Mekong Subregion 2030 and Beyond: Integration, Upgrading, Cities, and Connectivity*. To further explore these questions, this report discusses the existing production and trading structure of the Lao PDR in detail, as well as its position in the region.

It then explores interrelated pathways for achieving the country's development objectives and advancing the agenda of the GMS Program. This includes various upgrading pathways in and across economic sectors, including agriculture, services, and industry. It then discusses the potential for upgrading value chain positioning and the role of cities and connectivity infrastructure in supporting upgrading and diversification. Policy recommendations are provided in the conclusion.

Agriculture trade. Farmers load their produce for the market. The vegetables were grown using sustainable agricultural practices promoted by an ADB-supported project.

II

INTEGRATION OF THE LAO PDR INTO THE GREATER MEKONG SUBREGION AND THE GLOBAL ECONOMY

The Lao PDR is a strategically located small landlocked country, and is neighbor to major global trading partners. The total value of exports for 2016–2020 for the Lao PDR was $24.7 billion, including energy exports (Box 2). The value of imports for the same period was $25.9 billion. These numbers account for 0.03% and 0.03% of world exports and imports, respectively. Within the GMS countries, the Lao PDR accounts for a small fraction of total trade, at $21.7 billion or 1.7% of all GMS exports and $22.3 billion or 1.6% of all GMS imports during 2016–2020. Much of the GMS trade is dominated by the PRC, Thailand, and Viet Nam, with Cambodia, the Lao PDR, and Myanmar combined accounting for less than 2% of GMS exports and imports.

In terms of trade partners, the Lao PDR relies heavily on other GMS countries. The share of exports going to other GMS members is 87.3% for the Lao PDR (Figure 1). Imports by the Lao PDR are again dominated by trade with other GMS members. In the Lao PDR, 86.2% of imports come from other GMS economies (Figure 2).

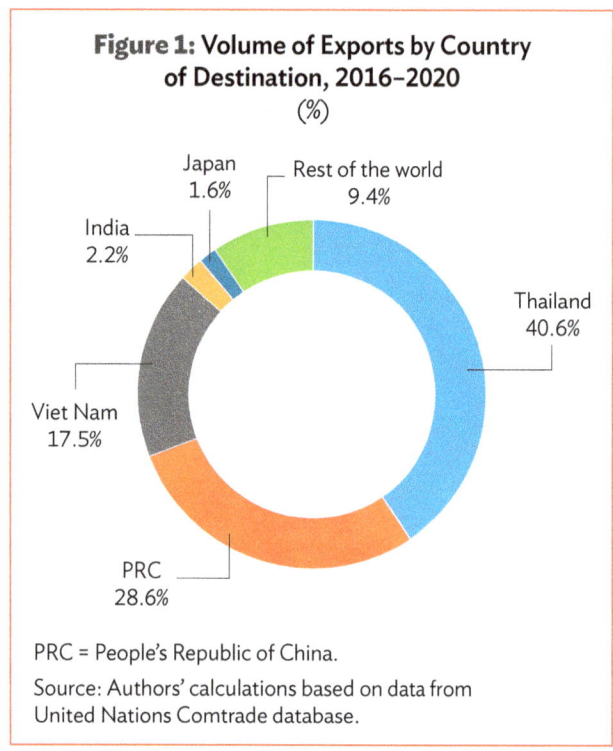

Figure 1: Volume of Exports by Country of Destination, 2016–2020 (%)

- Thailand 40.6%
- PRC 28.6%
- Viet Nam 17.5%
- India 2.2%
- Japan 1.6%
- Rest of the world 9.4%

PRC = People's Republic of China.
Source: Authors' calculations based on data from United Nations Comtrade database.

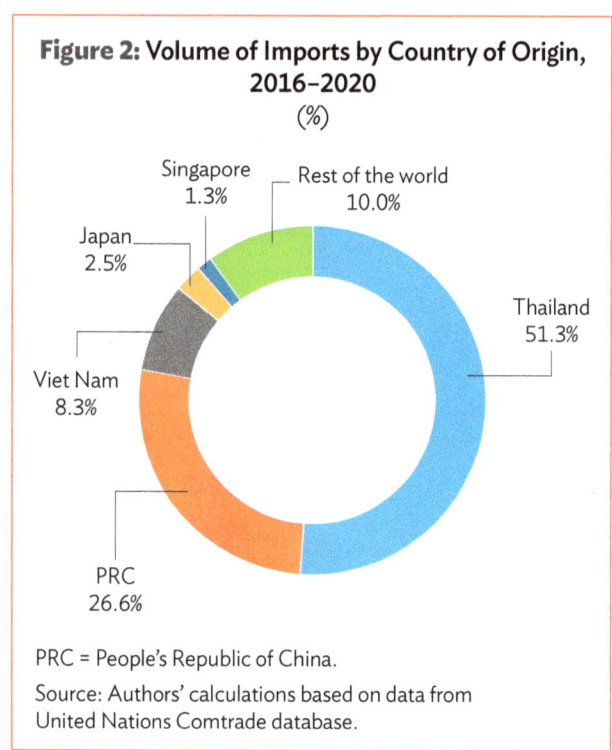

Figure 2: Volume of Imports by Country of Origin, 2016–2020 (%)

- Thailand 51.3%
- PRC 26.6%
- Viet Nam 8.3%
- Japan 2.5%
- Singapore 1.3%
- Rest of the world 10.0%

PRC = People's Republic of China.
Source: Authors' calculations based on data from United Nations Comtrade database.

Given the relative size of the Lao PDR's economy, it is the origin and destination of only a small share of total intra-GMS trade.

In terms of integration into world markets, this data implies that the Lao PDR has had limited success in increasing its trade with markets outside of the GMS. Much of the trade is also with middle-income economies rather than high-income economies. This has important implications on the effects of trade for development possibilities, as exporting to world markets provides opportunities to access wealthier economies and may have implications for the complexity of products produced domestically. On the import side, importing from more developed, high-income economies may provide access to more advanced technologies, which can encourage technology diffusion and aid technological upgrading.[3]

To summarize, the Lao PDR relies heavily on the GMS for both exports and imports, with limited expansion in trade with other countries in the global economy and limited change in trading partners over time. The relatively small shares of exports and imports between the Lao PDR and the rest of the world, and comparatively lower trade volumes with higher-income economies, reflects low demand and limited diversification of the country's production basket. There is thus great scope for expanding trade with regional and global partners that the Lao PDR trades with, including high-income countries in the context of global value chains (GVCs).

---

[3] ADB. 2021. *The Greater Mekong Subregion 2030 and Beyond: Integration, Upgrading, Cities, and Connectivity.* Manila.

Trade connectivity. Trucks and other vehicles pass through the Second Thai–Lao Friendship Bridge over the Mekong River, connecting Mukdahan Province in Thailand with Savannakhet in the Lao PDR. The bridge is 1.6 kms long and 12 meters wide and has two traffic lanes.

III

THE EXPORT STRUCTURE OF THE LAO PDR WITH THE GREATER MEKONG SUBREGION AND THE REST OF THE WORLD

The importance of a nation's production and export structures for its economic development has long been emphasized and established, particularly the diversity and uniqueness of products, as it can help to predict future growth.[4] Countries with a diversified and unique export basket are generally considered to be more complex. Becoming more diverse in production capabilities entails a process of economic upgrading. Upgrading one's production structure involves becoming more capital- and technology-intensive while also developing comparative advantages.

---

4   ADB. 2021. *The Greater Mekong Subregion 2030 and Beyond: Integration, Upgrading, Cities, and Connectivity.* Manila.

Three sectors account for almost half of the exports of GMS members: capital electronics, consumer textiles, and intermediate electronics. Electronics, whether capital or intermediate, require a high level of production capabilities, while consumer textiles require significantly lower production capabilities than electronics. In comparison, the Lao PDR's top three export sectors are other goods (mostly electricity exports), mining, and basic metals (Figure 3). These products are associated with lower levels of production capabilities when compared to the top three exports of all GMS countries. However, the Lao PDR has experienced a high degree of structural change in its export composition since 1996–2020 (Figure 4). Consumer textiles exports declined as competition for this market increased globally, while energy exports rose, along with mining and basic metal exports, as the government pursued its development aspiration of becoming the "Battery of Asia" (Box 2).

More recently, progress has been made in export of electronics and electrical equipment from special economic zones that participate in GVCs, as well as in export of food and beverages. The country's export basket, nonetheless, remains much less-diversified than in other countries in the GMS. This is represented through a comparatively low number of products that it exports and with its export structure dominated by products associated with primary and low-technology sectors. In sum, the Lao PDR's economy still highly depends on a small number of capital-intensive commodity exports for its growth, with the current export structure's capacity to generate quality jobs for driving poverty reduction constrained.

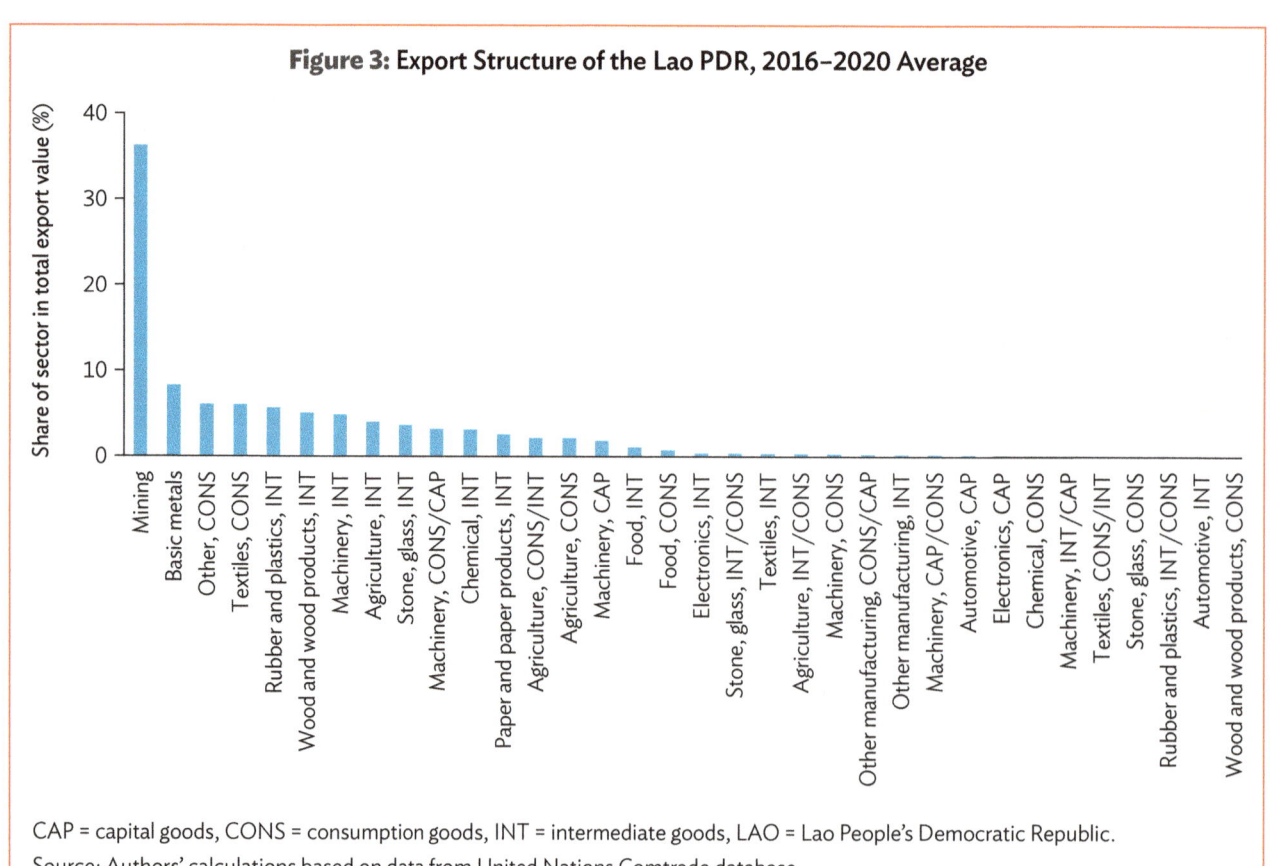

Figure 3: Export Structure of the Lao PDR, 2016–2020 Average

CAP = capital goods, CONS = consumption goods, INT = intermediate goods, LAO = Lao People's Democratic Republic.
Source: Authors' calculations based on data from United Nations Comtrade database.

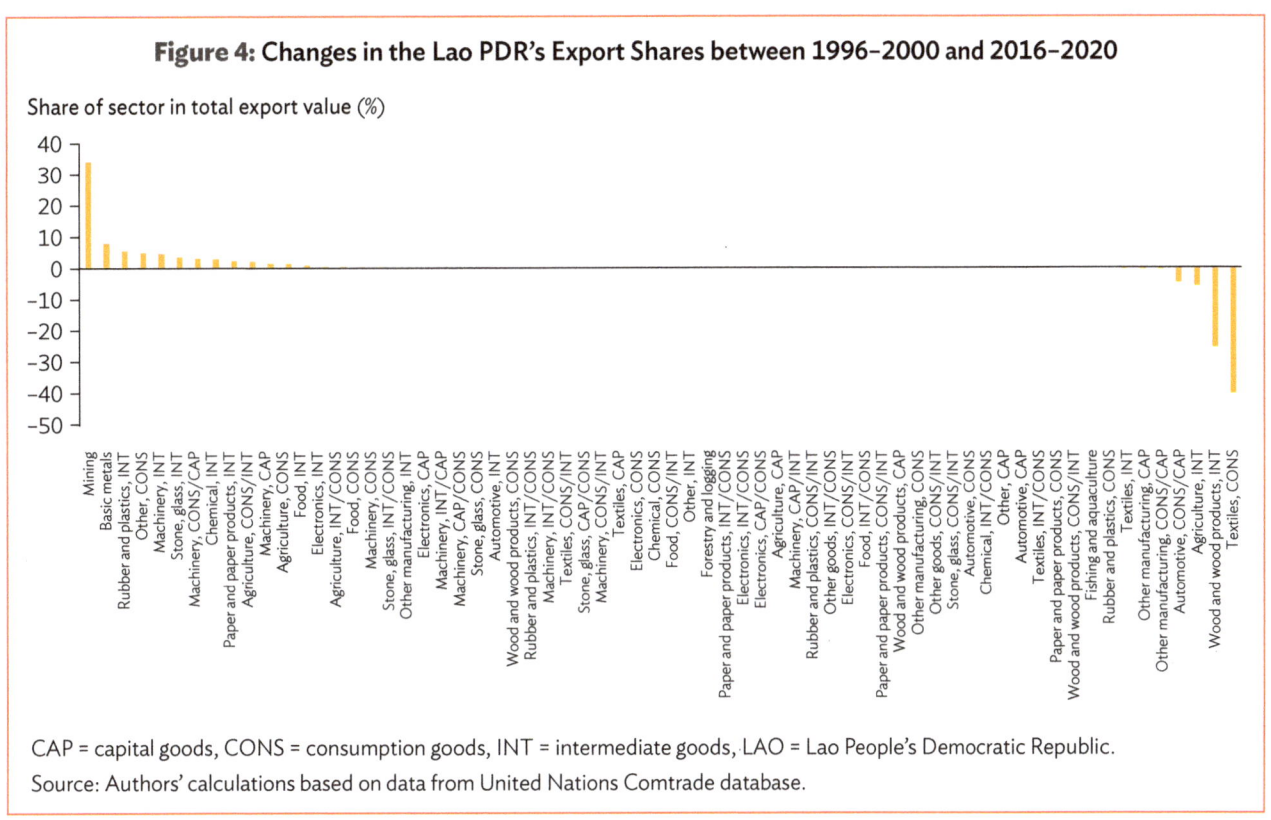

Figure 4: Changes in the Lao PDR's Export Shares between 1996–2000 and 2016–2020

CAP = capital goods, CONS = consumption goods, INT = intermediate goods, LAO = Lao People's Democratic Republic.
Source: Authors' calculations based on data from United Nations Comtrade database.

Box 2: Clean Battery of Asia

The Lao People's Democratic Republic (Lao PDR) has enjoyed robust economic expansion over 2 decades, fueled by investment in the country's hydropower sector. Gross domestic product (GDP) growth averaged above 7.0% between 2000 and 2019, boosted by investments that tap the country's hydroelectric potential to realize the government's development aspiration of becoming the "Battery of Asia." The Lao PDR's electricity sector significantly contributes to the economy and the country's export earnings. The power generation subsector accounts for approximately 10% of the country's GDP, with electricity exports accounting for one-third of total exports. This energy is sent to countries including Thailand, Cambodia, Myanmar, the People's Republic of China, and Viet Nam. The government also earns revenues derived from taxes, royalties, and dividends from entities involved in power generation estimated at 1.0% of GDP. More broadly the country benefits from foreign investment in the subsector, with one-third of the country's foreign direct investment going to electricity infrastructure. Power exports could increase to 50 terawatt-hours by 2030.

Strong foreign investment inflows are expected to continue to support the development and supply of low-carbon electricity, storage, and grid connectivity in the Lao PDR for export markets. As of 2022, wind farm investments of 1.6 gigawatts are planned, including the 600-megawatt (MW) Monsoon Wind project in the Xekong and Attapeu provinces that will export energy to Viet Nam. These investments will turn the project into one of the world's largest wind farms and save 90 million tons of carbon throughout the project's lifespan. With the Lao PDR planning to increase the share of solar power in its energy mix to almost 25% by 2025, an investment project of 240 MW floating solar at Nam Theun 2 has been proposed. Keppel Electric and Electricite Du Laos are formulating a joint venture to import renewable hydropower as part of Singapore's green energy 2030 ambitions. The completion of eight additional hydropower projects in 2022 and 2023, with total installed capacity of 1,500 MW, will also help meet demand for export of the Lao PDR's renewable energy to the region.

Sources: Authors' calculations; ADB. 2019. *Lao People's Democratic Republic Energy Sector Assessment, Strategy, and Road Map*. Manila.

However, the goods the Lao PDR exports to its GMS neighbors are more diverse than those it exports to the rest of the world. This may provide opportunities to develop global competitiveness by building on improvements in regional competitiveness. That is, there are potential pathways for diversification and industrialization via greater regional cooperation and regional competition. As knowledge tends to diffuse more easily across relatively short distances, countries that are geographically close to each other, such as those in the GMS, may develop shared production and export capabilities. Knowledge also tends to diffuse more easily across similar product types. The Lao PDR's export of basic metals, electronics, and chemicals form part of regional value chains, and therefore, these exports have potential to benefit from market and technology development opportunities. Being surrounded by neighbors that invest in improving their capabilities presents an opportunity for diversification and upgrading for the Lao PDR. It may therefore be advantageous to support greater coordination of regional policies on capabilities development for improving comparative advantages.

An important question, therefore, is how to encourage the spread of capabilities, technology, knowledge, and network linkages between GMS neighboring countries to support per capita growth spillovers. Factors that may influence outcomes include structural barriers related to the integration of the Lao PDR into the regional and global economy, participation, and positioning in GVCs, existing capabilities, and the quality of regional cooperation and integration in the GMS. This can be examined through understanding interrelations between the destinations of the Lao PDR's exports and its neighboring countries as well as how this may interact with trends related to GMS countries' per capita growth rate.

Analysis finds a positive correlation between the Lao PDR's per capita GDP growth and that of its neighbors. This is because the Lao PDR relies heavily on its neighbors as a market for its exports. Figure 5 illustrates clearly that over 87.3% of the Lao PDR's exports go to neighboring GMS countries. More broadly, for the GMS countries, an increase in the per capita growth rate by 1 percentage point is associated with an increase in per capita GDP growth of 0.4 percentage points in neighboring countries.[5] This finding highlights that regional integration and cooperation has an important role to play in the growth performance of the GMS countries, with its members benefiting from per capita growth spillovers from one another. Such spillovers help to promote convergence. A caveat is that the Lao PDR's energy exports, which account for a large share of total exports, do not necessarily offer the same contribution to product sophistication and market development as other types of manufactured products.

The Lao PDR's greater reliance on spillovers from its neighbors is also indicative of a less-diversified export structure and that it has met its export potential with most GMS members (Table 2). Analysis of export potential finds that given the Lao PDR's current export structure, the only trading partner in the GMS that remains unexploited is Myanmar. Opportunities do however exist in other products and outside the GMS countries. This highlights the importance of upgrading production, including through leveraging benefits from regional cooperation, to increase interaction with the global economy for opening new opportunities associated with unexploited export potential in new markets. One way to achieve this is for the Lao PDR to participate in the regional and global production networks and value chains.

---

[5] ADB. 2021. *The Greater Mekong Subregion 2030 and Beyond: Integration, Upgrading, Cities, and Connectivity*. Manila.

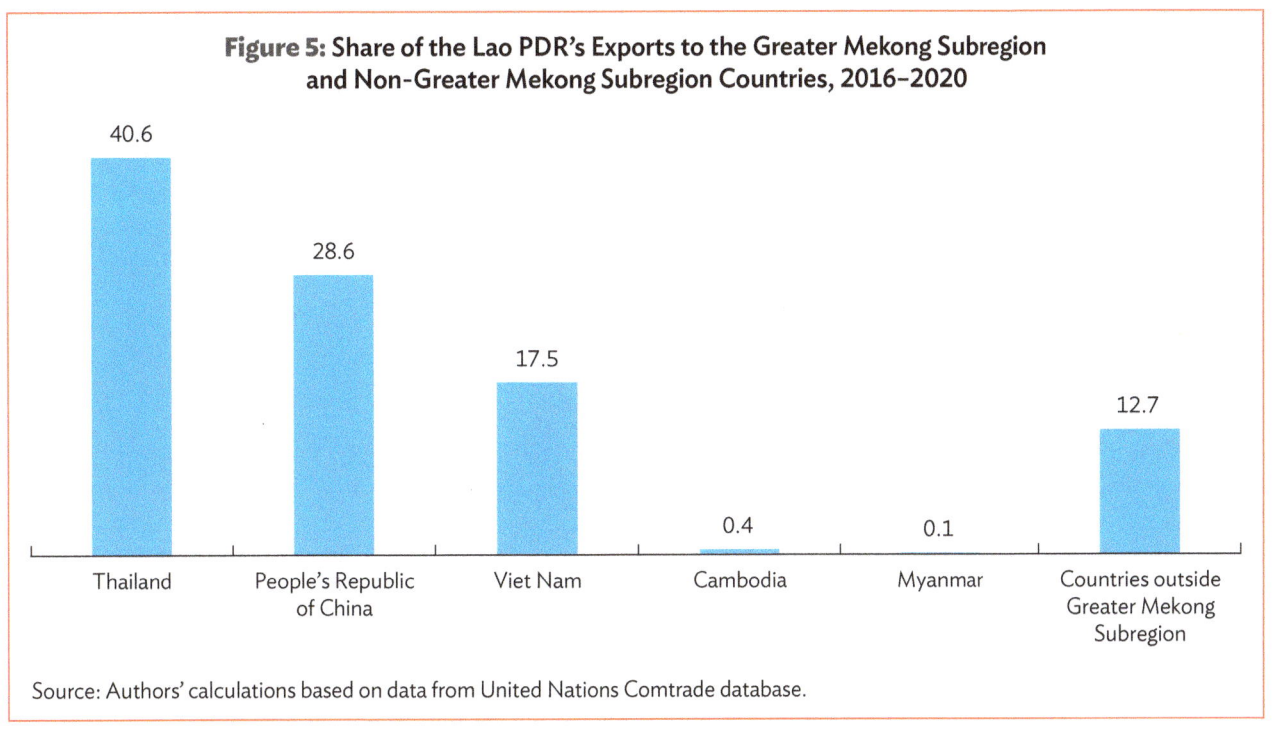

Figure 5: Share of the Lao PDR's Exports to the Greater Mekong Subregion and Non–Greater Mekong Subregion Countries, 2016–2020

Source: Authors' calculations based on data from United Nations Comtrade database.

Table 2: Unexploited Export Potential within the Greater Mekong Subregion

Economies	Cambodia	Lao PDR	Myanmar	PRC	Thailand	Viet Nam
Cambodia						
Lao PDR	High		High			
Myanmar	High	High				
PRC	High				High	High
Thailand	High			High		High
Viet Nam	High		High	High	High	

Lao PDR = Lao People's Democratic Republic, PRC = People's Republic of China.

Notes: Orange is indicated for the Lao PDR. A blank white cell indicates that the country is meeting its export potential with its trade partner, while "High" indicates a relative residual above 30 (representing high export potential).

Source: ADB. 2021. *The Greater Mekong Subregion 2030 and Beyond: Integration, Upgrading, Cities, and Connectivity*. Manila.

Skills upgrading. Technicians and workers assemble electronic products at one of the factories in the Savan Park Special Economic Zone in Savannakhet. The growth of industry and cross-border trade is creating jobs in the area. ADB supported the training of Lao officials to manage the zone and promote its attractions to foreign investors.

IV

STRUCTURAL TRANSFORMATION: DIVERSIFICATION AND UPGRADING

Economic development entails a process of transformation of the activities taking place in the economy, especially in terms of the complexity of tasks undertaken by workers and enterprises. That is, workers and the self-employed leave subsistence agriculture and informal low-end services to move into higher productivity and higher wage activities in all sectors across the economy. Transformation takes place by developing new capabilities, which allow producers and service providers to sell new products and services in foreign markets.[6]

When the range of capabilities in a country expands over time, the portfolio of products and services that the country exports will also expand. This is called diversification. At the same time, it is expected that the new products and services will embody more knowledge and become unique or sophisticated. This process of developing new capabilities aimed at producing and exporting more sophisticated products and services is referred to as upgrading. As capabilities accumulate, the development of new capabilities opens new options for upgrading. New capabilities include expanding and harnessing the productivity of all members of society. In this situation there may be an opportunity to make further progress on gender equality given that employment in such areas may be

---

[6] ADB. 2021. *The Greater Mekong Subregion 2030 and Beyond: Integration, Upgrading, Cities, and Connectivity.* Manila.

more suitable for women. Women in Lao PDR still lack sufficient access to knowledge, entrepreneurial skills training, and finance, which often results in them being tied to low-waged, unpaid, and routine jobs. Box 3 discusses opportunities for addressing these issues in the context of the GMS regional cooperation program.

The Lao PDR exports products with comparative low levels of knowledge and complexity. Therefore, opportunities for upgrading in the short-term are mostly in other products that have low or medium complexity. However, it is important to initiate new economic policies to support a shift toward increasing product complexity, as such policies are likely to provide an environment for the establishment of longer-term positive relationships between the complexity of product services with the income of workers and enterprises. That is, more complex products are associated with higher wages and higher productivity.

As discussed in section III, the Lao PDR's economy has a comparatively low level of diversification. Its largest export sector is "other consumer products," which is mainly electricity (Figure 3). Other important export sectors are mining and intermediate chemicals. The product complexity scores of these sectors are generally below the global average. Figure 6 shows that there are only four sectors where the Lao PDR produces goods that have product complexity scores higher than the global average, with fabricated metal capital goods and other transport capital equipment having the highest product complexity. Closer examination of transport production activities by product indicates that such manufacturing in country is dominated by assembly of imported parts and accessories for vehicles in the local market. Therefore, even in comparatively complex sectors, the activities undertaken in the Lao PDR lack sophistication. As such, measures to boost non-resource exports are a priority.

Box 3: Gender Equality and the Greater Mekong Subregion Economic Cooperation Program

The need for economic empowerment of women has been recognized by the Greater Mekong Subregion (GMS) Economic Cooperation Program (GMS-2030), and its members, including the Lao People's Democratic Republic (Lao PDR). For example, the Lao PDR has introduced laws and regulations to promote the advancement of women, including the 2020 promulgation of the Law on Gender Equality, commitment to the objectives of the Committee on the Elimination of Discrimination against Women, and establishment of the Lao National Commission for the Advancement of Women, Mothers and Children.

These actions have resulted in improvements in the Lao PDR's positioning on global gender equality indexes, such as the World Economic Forum's Global Gender Gap Index where the country climbed to 43rd from 52nd place in 2020. However, weak implementation of regulatory commitments has seen inequalities persist. Women are more likely to work informally and there is a significant gender gap in enterprise ownership, both of which affect the quality of women's participation in the private sector. Disparities in education attainment persists between genders, with this associated with lower earning potential later in life.

The GMS, as an open platform, provides an ideal forum for countries and stakeholders to share gender-responsive practices and work together to advance gender equality. The objectives of the GMS Gender Strategy are to (i) improve existing, and develop new innovative approaches to gender mainstreaming activities to ensure equal access and participation in program-related activities; (ii) complement subregional efforts to explicitly address gender-based barriers affecting the full participation of individuals of all ages, abilities, in all socioeconomic spheres; and (iii) address pervasive gender norms that disadvantage one group over another.

Source: ADB. 2022. *Greater Mekong Subregion Gender Strategy*. Manila.

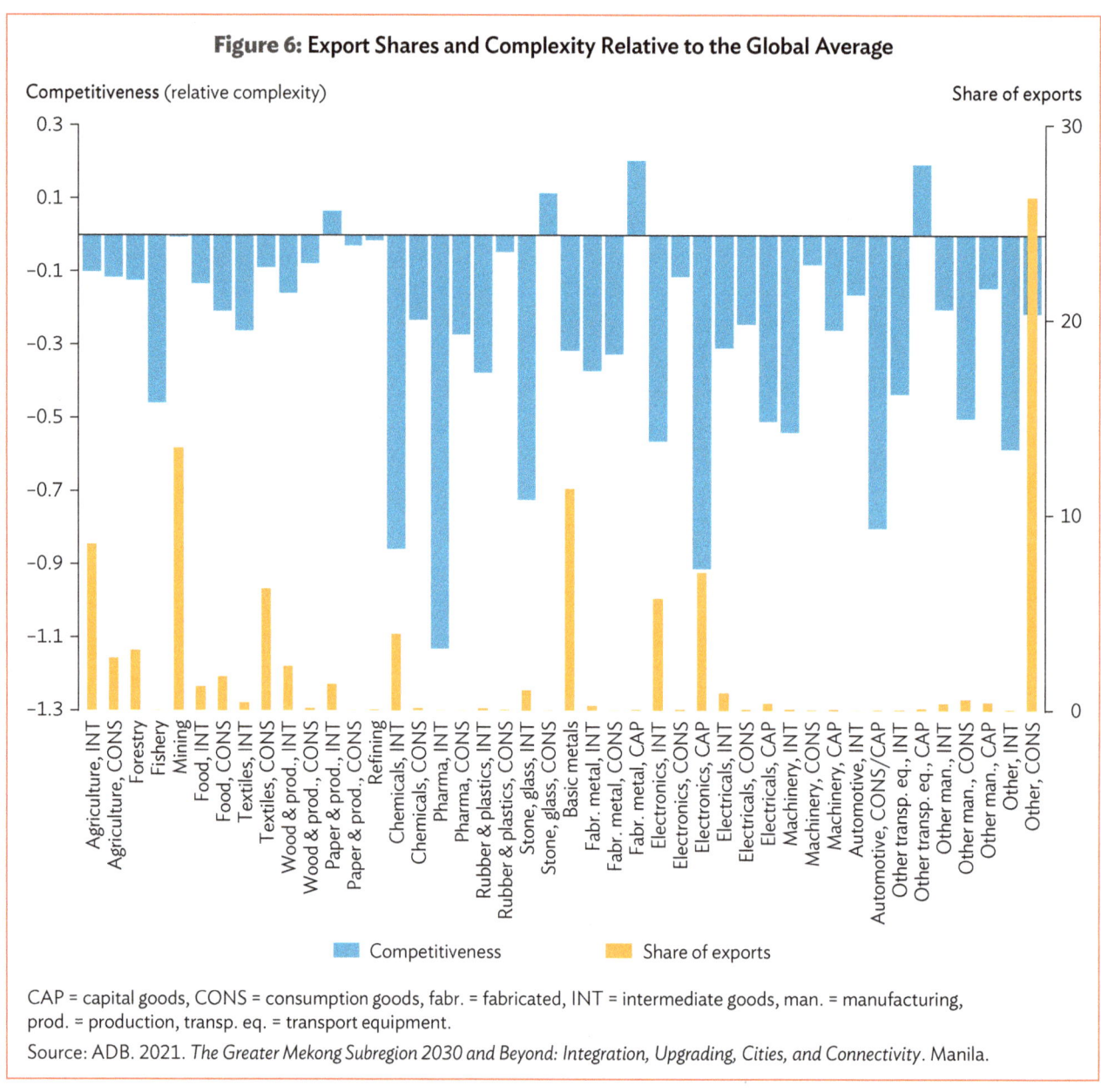

Figure 6: Export Shares and Complexity Relative to the Global Average

CAP = capital goods, CONS = consumption goods, fabr. = fabricated, INT = intermediate goods, man. = manufacturing, prod. = production, transp. eq. = transport equipment.
Source: ADB. 2021. *The Greater Mekong Subregion 2030 and Beyond: Integration, Upgrading, Cities, and Connectivity*. Manila.

Therefore, the question is how to accelerate the process of upgrading and diversification, including for greater integration in the global economy. An important element of this is understanding the products and services that are likely to be good targets for improving the Lao PDR's capabilities and complexity for structural transformation of the economy. The ease or difficulty in obtaining comparative advantage is related to complexity and current capabilities. The more complex the sector or product, the greater the effort to achieve comparative advantage. Figure 7 is a graphic presentation of a conceptual framework for the process of structural transformation. The conceptual framework involves two dimensions: (i) potential upgrading gain, and (ii) upgrading relatedness. **Potential upgrading gain** involves understanding the group of products that the Lao PDR is exporting with and without comparative advantage. This latter group comprises the set of potential products. **Upgrading relatedness** involves understanding how these "potential products" are related to the products that are currently produced with comparative advantage.

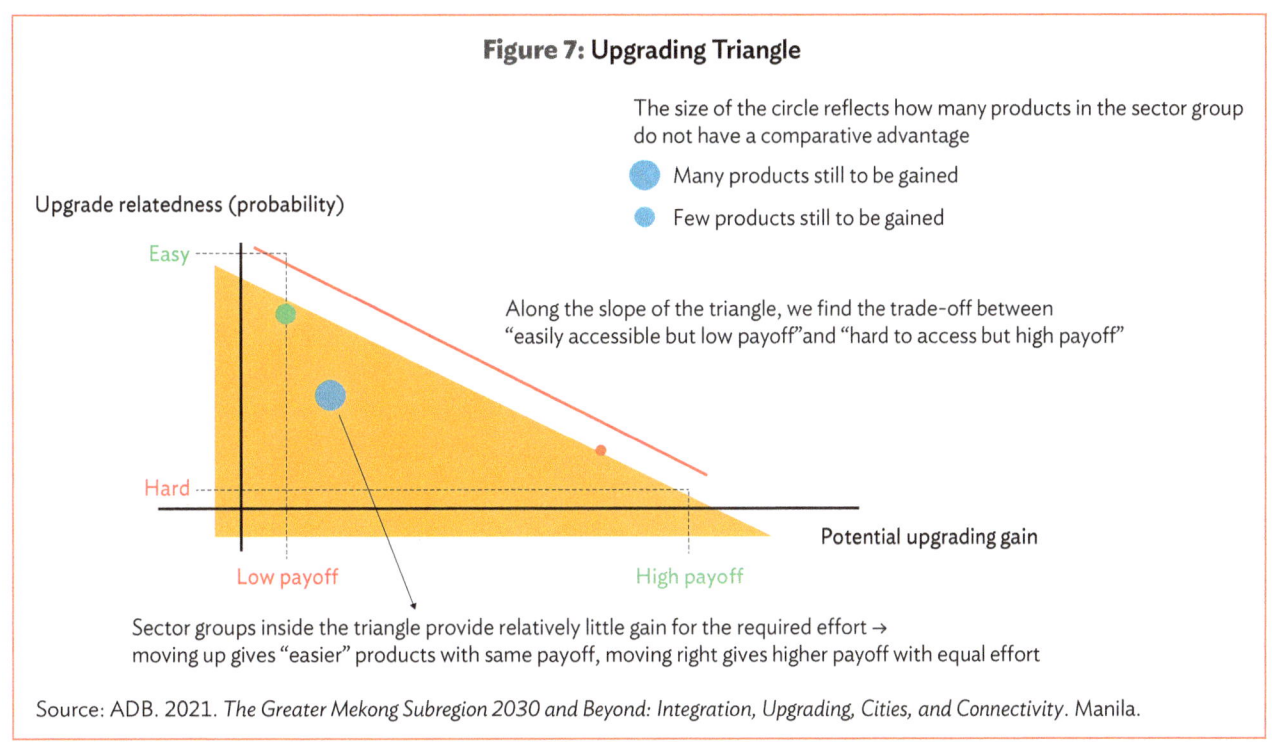

Figure 7: Upgrading Triangle

Source: ADB. 2021. *The Greater Mekong Subregion 2030 and Beyond: Integration, Upgrading, Cities, and Connectivity*. Manila.

A high level of **upgrading relatedness** implies that the potential products are relatively accessible, making it easier to gain comparative advantage. This is a short step. Meanwhile a high level of **potential upgrading gain** implies that the product is relatively difficult to master, but that it has a higher payoff once comparative advantage is obtained. This is a strategic bet.

Sectors that tend to be easy to move into also tend to be less complex and offer lower financial gains. In comparison, sectors that offer larger financial gains tend to be harder to enter. Here, policy makers need to think about issues related to volume and value. According to this methodology, the "best" approach for the Lao PDR is to target those sectors and products that appear along the edge of the triangle. That is, those with the highest ease of obtaining comparative advantage or the highest payoff gains.

Policy makers also need to decide the speed that they want to move wages and income per capita in the coming decades. Equitable increases in income per capita will only occur if significant shares of workers shift their production toward more complex products and services where remuneration and wages are higher. This means that economic policy and national plans should focus on the idea of new production possibilities as a central goal of the development strategy. Furthermore, as firms will undertake these activities, significant coordination between the public and private sectors is needed. Enterprises need to be aware of opportunities and how to acquire the necessary capabilities. Such information and questions are important topics for public–private dialogues.[7] This can increase awareness of private sector firms on potential opportunities and provide valuable insights into regulatory bottlenecks and appropriate policy interventions for governments. Government policy and public–private dialogues play a critical role in the success of structural transformation efforts.

---

[7] ADB. 2021. *The Greater Mekong Subregion 2030 and Beyond: Integration, Upgrading, Cities, and Connectivity*. Manila.

Backing business. Workers work at an organic fertilizer factory in the Hatsayfong district of Vientiane. The need for fertilizer has increased as the growth in border trade increases demand for agricultural products from the Lao PDR. ADB supported the improvement of the business environment to enable local people to establish their micro, small, and medium-sized enterprises to boost trade, employment, and income.

V

DIVERSIFYING AND UPGRADING: CAPABILITIES FOR NEW AND MORE COMPLEX PRODUCTS

This section applies the methodology introduced in section IV to construct the upgrading triangle to support export diversification for the Lao PDR, including potential short-run gains. The products or sectors highlighted in this section may be discussed by policy makers and the private sector in their dialogue about the future of the Lao PDR economy. Policy dialogue on how to create an enabling environment for specific products can be helpful for identifying a broad range of measures, be they general or narrow, to support the development of new industries to drive the process of structural transformation.

Figure 8 shows the short-run upgrading triangle. Subsectors highlighted in green represent opportunities with high upgrading relatedness in the short run. These include consumer textiles products, along with other manufacturing products and consumer paper and products. These sectors are accessible but have lower gains to offer. The sectors that are more difficult to enter but that offer higher gains are in orange. These sectors include consumer-fabricated metal, consumer electrical products, and other intermediate manufactured products. In the longer term, there are many new sectors into which the Lao PDR could upgrade and diversify. However, long-run upgrading opportunities depend upon how successful the country is in achieving the short-run gains that are on offer.

Diversifying and Upgrading: Capabilities for New and More Complex Products

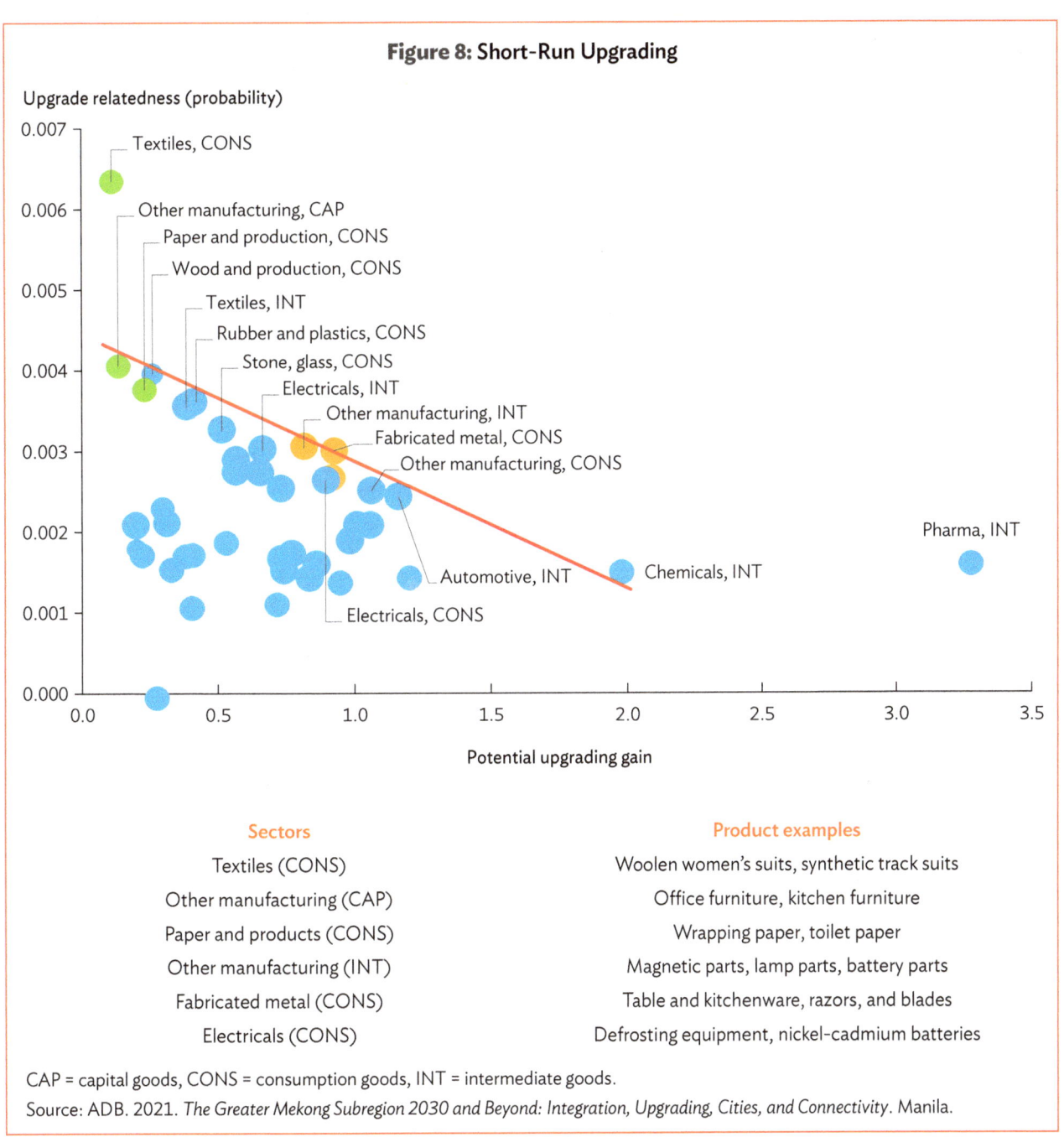

Figure 8: Short-Run Upgrading

CAP = capital goods, CONS = consumption goods, INT = intermediate goods.
Source: ADB. 2021. *The Greater Mekong Subregion 2030 and Beyond: Integration, Upgrading, Cities, and Connectivity*. Manila.

The illustration provided in the upgrading triangles presents the idea of shared production capabilities between products and sectors. The presence of a shared production capability entails that an upgrading opportunity is more easily accessible than if it was not present. It provides a useful perspective on upgrading, highlighting that production capabilities are shared among products. As comparative advantage is gained in new products, more opportunities to diversify will become available. For example, the development of wig manufacturing in the Republic of Korea in the 1960s supported accumulation of capabilities that were transferable to other labor-intensive industries.

This is important for consideration in medium-term and long-term planning, particularly as various information and coordination failures can hinder the speed of progress on diversifying and upgrading toward more complex activities. Moving the production structure toward more complex processes for progressing structural transformation means competing on quality rather than price. It also requires investment and greater human capital accumulation among workers. Dialogue between public and private sectors can help to identify specific constraints that cause coordination failures and information asymmetries. Such dialogue can help to identify appropriate solutions to address these issues.

Upgrading is representative of a road map for development that will create better-quality employment and increase incomes. To realize potential, the private sector will have to invest in new capabilities. Public policy regulations should provide an environment to enable this. Policy and the upgrading path also need to comprehensively involve all factors that support production, including human capital and the training of workers, education and vocational training providers, entrepreneurship incubation, export promotion, and investment in knowledge and capital infrastructure.

In addition to limited human capital and low-technology adoption, bottlenecks to private sector growth, and in product upgrading and diversification, are often due to the inefficiency of public institutions and weak governance. Shortfalls in institutional quality mean that there are substantial issues in the business environment and lack of mechanisms to address the information and coordination asymmetries. Efforts are needed to strengthen public–private dialogue, including for identifying specific actions to build strong institutions.

Climate resilient agriculture. Farmers benefit from the upgrading of irrigation and water control infrastructure for better water supply management to enhance productivity under flood and drought conditions.

VI UPGRADING PATHS: AGRICULTURE

Demand for the Lao PDR's agriculture exports has been robust, but much of these exports—particularly fruit and vegetables—do not currently involve processing. Many agricultural smallholders have also transitioned from subsistence agriculture to contract farming of production crops, such as cassava, bananas, and coffee, much of which is exported to regional and global markets. With the spread of agricultural commercialization and cross-border agriculture, farm incomes have increased, and poverty rates have declined.[8] Over time the share of agricultural employment in the total workforce has also declined, from 80% in 2000 to approximately 60% in 2020 (Figure 9), but it is still among the highest in Asia. Few are engaged in more complex and high value segments of agriculture, such as commercial livestock and fisheries or agro-processing. In addition, agricultural product and market chains are dominated by own-account workers or small groups that operate as agriculture enterprises, limiting the sector's productivity growth and participation in value chains.

While agriculture is an important source of livelihood and a driver of poverty reduction for the poorest rural households in the Lao PDR, the current structure of the sector contains relatively few opportunities for significant upgrading. Similarly, capabilities in agriculture may provide relatively limited support for moving into more complex activities into nonagriculture sectors. Therefore, greater effort should be made to modernize agriculture, particularly through new climate-smart technologies, and shift toward more complex segments of agricultural production and commercialization as well as agro-processing. Quality certifications and compliance with sanitary and phytosanitary standards would also support efforts to lift agricultural exports and related products to trade partners.

---

[8] World Bank. 2022. *Linking Laos, Unlocking Policies. Lao PDR Country Economic Memorandum*. Washington, DC.

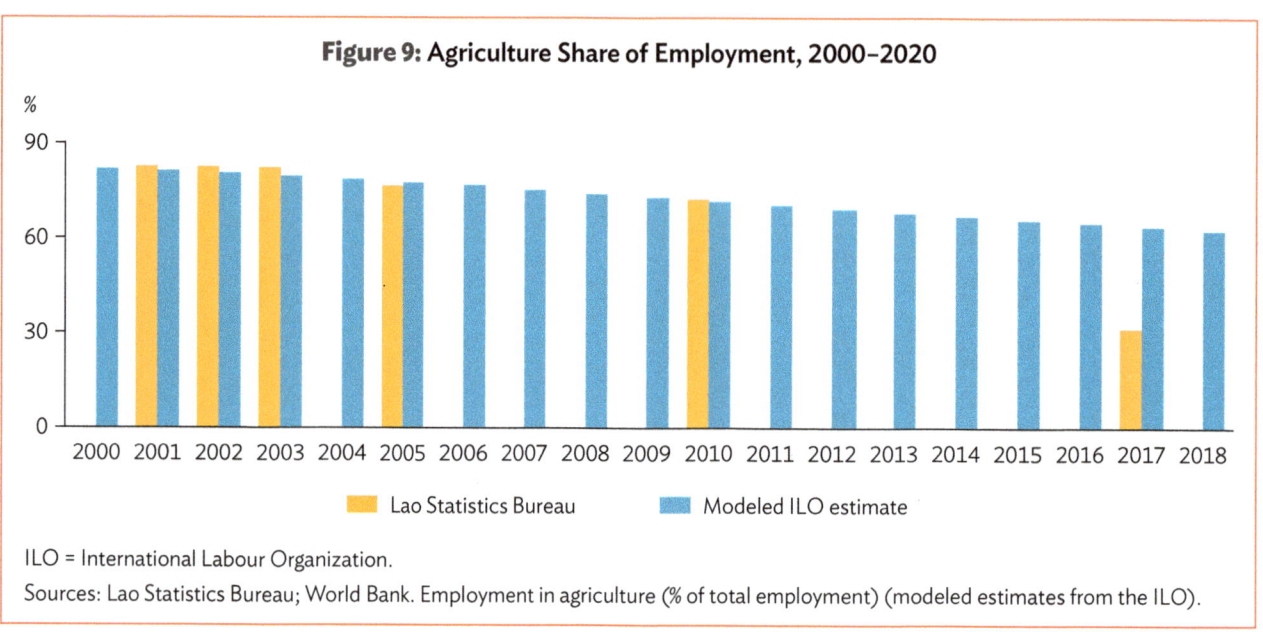

Figure 9: Agriculture Share of Employment, 2000–2020

ILO = International Labour Organization.
Sources: Lao Statistics Bureau; World Bank. Employment in agriculture (% of total employment) (modeled estimates from the ILO).

Given the importance of agriculture as a source of gross value added, and especially of employment in the Lao PDR, it is important to consider the upgrading possibilities that exist within this sector. Sectors that appear to have high upgrade-probability opportunities in the Lao PDR are highlighted in green on Figure 10 and include coffee, tea, and cocoa; dairy and honey; plants and flowers. Rubber, highlighted in orange, offers a higher complexity gain. There is also space to capture greater market share in organic products, with the current share of land dedicated to organic farming still small. Furthermore, increasing demand in Asia for protein may provide opportunities for increasing livestock and fisheries production for export.

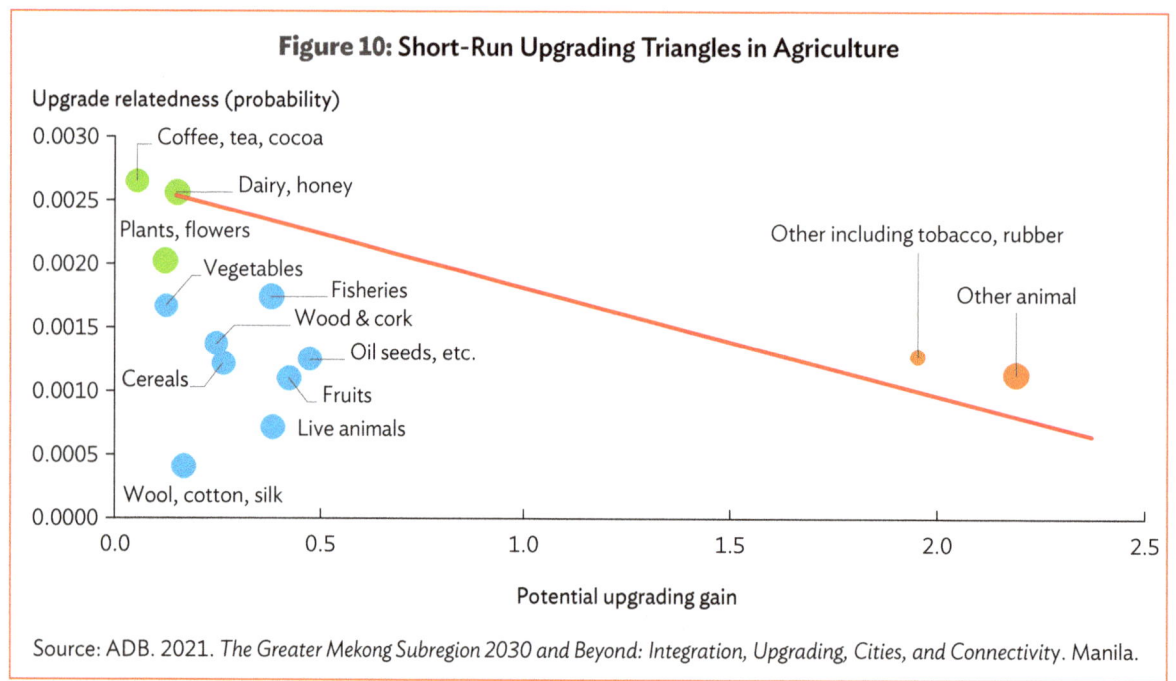

Figure 10: Short-Run Upgrading Triangles in Agriculture

Source: ADB. 2021. *The Greater Mekong Subregion 2030 and Beyond: Integration, Upgrading, Cities, and Connectivity*. Manila.

However, studies identify several constraints to agriculture sector development in the Lao PDR, including access to finance, infrastructure quality, access to competitive markets and value chains, land tenure, and incentives for innovation (Box 4). The low number of graduates from agriculture-related courses as well as limited research and development in this sector is a constraint. Underdeveloped agriculture value chains and commercial networks contribute to difficulty in accessing inputs, credit, technology, know-how, and markets, which in turn limits productivity and income. Prices remain depressed due to issues in maintaining product quality across numerous actors, including farmers, traders, processors, retailers, and exporters. These issues also limit the commercialization potential of agricultural products.

Box 4: Agriculture Development Is Essential for Structural Transformation and Inclusive Growth

A lack of productivity growth in the agriculture sector explains much of the stalled structural transformation of the Lao People's Democratic Republic (Lao PDR). The global experience is that agricultural growth is a necessary precedent for the structural transformation process, and that agricultural growth has two to three times the poverty-reducing effect of nonagricultural growth. This is especially so when agriculture employs a large share of the population. In the Lao PDR, agriculture accounts for 60% of national employment and it provides the livelihoods for majority of the poor. A substantial share of the agricultural population remains at the subsistence level. Reducing poverty depends on helping this population to become commercially oriented and connected to the market economy.

Agricultural potential is high but remains untapped. With extensive land area relative to its rural population, abundant water resources, and proximity to growing food markets, the Lao PDR could have large potential for agricultural development. By many measures, conditions in the Lao PDR are among the most favorable in Asia. However, the investments necessary to make use of this potential have largely not yet occurred. Agriculture has not received a proportionate share of public investment, and majority of agricultural investment has been development assistance. This means that agricultural performance has remained limited and as a result, progress on food security and poverty reduction have stalled.

Clear constraints explain the low performance of agriculture to date. Although the Lao PDR has the highest level of renewable water resources available per unit of agricultural land in Asia, irrigation coverage remains among the lowest in the region. Input and output markets remain fragmented and underdeveloped, and credit is highly constrained. Road infrastructure and logistics performance trail most of Asia. Investment in research and extension systems to underpin innovation is at low levels. Most farmers also operate without legally recognized land-use rights, which makes the investment climate for agriculture unfavorable.

Targeted public investments in the agriculture sector can make a difference to development outcomes. Irrigation improvement, particularly through small-scale and community-managed irrigation, is essential to make use of the Lao PDR's abundant water resources. Rural road infrastructure and credit are essential to achieving agricultural diversification outcomes. Secure land-use rights and land-use planning also reduce agricultural encroachment into natural ecosystems and support crop diversification. New technologies contribute to productivity, but extension system reforms are needed to backstop this process. The effectiveness of these investments can be further enhanced by investing in knowledge infrastructure, statistical systems to inform policy, and policies that facilitate, rather than restrict, trade.

Source: ADB. 2017. *Lao PDR: Accelerating Structural Transformation for Inclusive Growth—Country Diagnostic Study*. Manila.

Luangnamtha airport. Upgraded in 2012 to boost trade and tourism.

VII

UPGRADING PATHS: SERVICES

In recent times, there have been concerns that the process of "servicification," entailing an accelerated rise in the economies of the services sectors, began earlier in the process of structural transformation. Over the past 2 decades, the services sector dominated the Lao PDR economy and has remained stable at comparatively high levels (Figure 11). Hence, the services sector was the largest contributor to economic growth during this time. Following this, the services share of employment rose from 11% in 1991–1993 to 25% in 2017–2019. However, the sectoral employment share remains low compared to other countries in Southeast Asia (Figure 12).

Breaking down services into its nine subsectors reveals that wholesale and retail trade accounts for the largest share of the sector's contribution to GDP, followed by transport and storage (Figure 13). While these sectors have provided job opportunities, they tend to have lower wages and lower levels of productivity when compared to more complex services sectors such as financial services and information and communication technology. The Lao PDR's services sector, therefore, is still in its early stage of development, with the country still needing to develop modern services as well as upgrade traditional services.

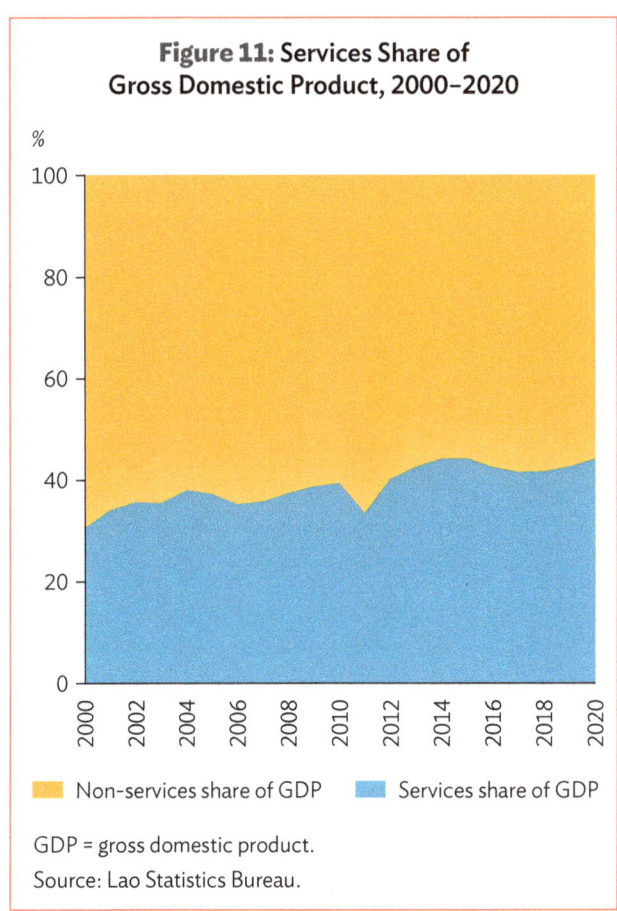

Figure 11: Services Share of Gross Domestic Product, 2000–2020

GDP = gross domestic product.
Source: Lao Statistics Bureau.

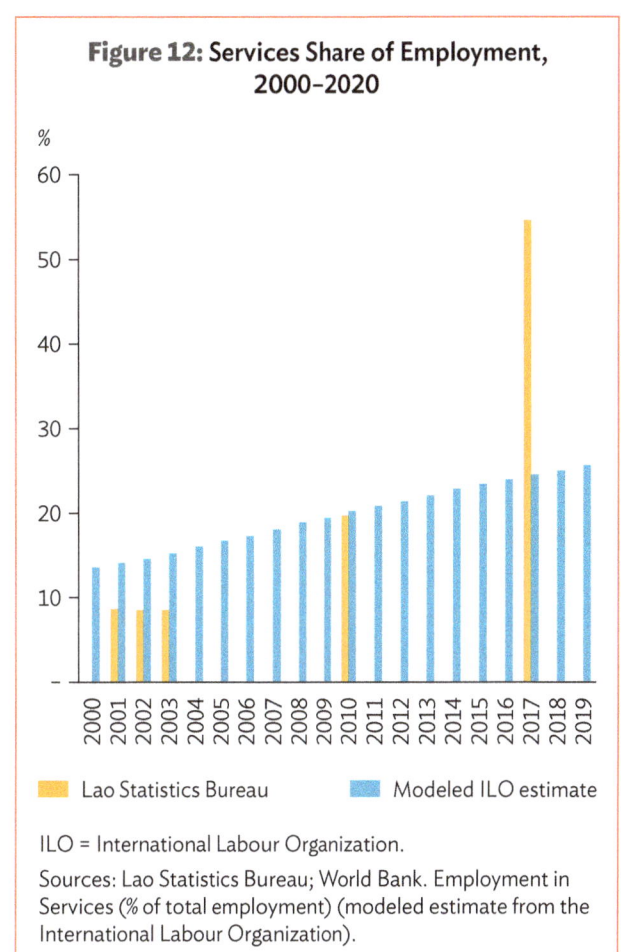

Figure 12: Services Share of Employment, 2000–2020

ILO = International Labour Organization.
Sources: Lao Statistics Bureau; World Bank. Employment in Services (% of total employment) (modeled estimate from the International Labour Organization).

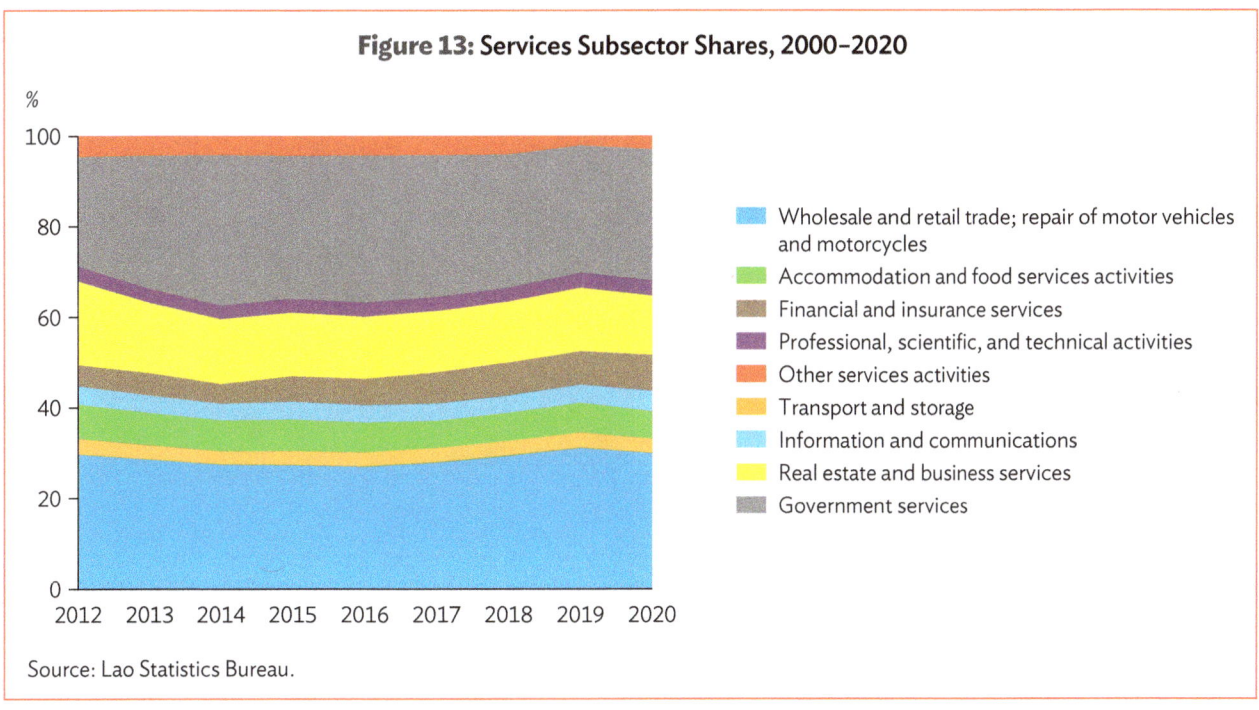

Figure 13: Services Subsector Shares, 2000–2020

Source: Lao Statistics Bureau.

The lackluster development of the services sector is also illustrated through its declining share in total exports, which averaged 25% between 2001–2010 and fell to an average of 15% between 2011–2020 (Figure 14). Services exports related to tourism industries have featured dominantly, with international tourism receipts a major source of foreign exchange earnings. While tourism is an important source of exports and employment, the Lao PDR's tourism economy is characterized by a comparatively low spend per tourist and short visit durations. Policy should focus on upgrading the quality of tourism-related services (Box 5), while also diversifying and expanding its services exports into more advanced areas such as financial and business services. Tourism has a potential to act as a much more powerful driver of inclusive growth, including through improved synergies with tourism destinations in other GMS countries. Support for skills upgrading, such as through hospitality management schools, may be useful for supporting the upgrading of tourism-related industries.

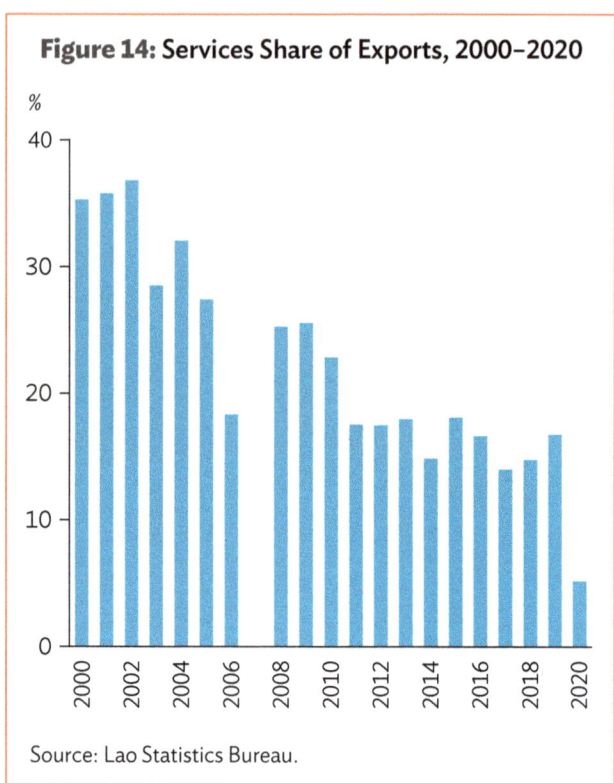

Figure 14: Services Share of Exports, 2000–2020

Source: Lao Statistics Bureau.

Box 5: Building Tourism Competitiveness

The Lao People's Democratic Republic (Lao PDR) has been steadily diversifying its services sector by improving the business environment and growing tourism, while increasing the use of technology. However, the pandemic changed the course of the economy. The tourism sector suffered, but digital services thrived. Despite the uptick in technology adoption among the population, the majority of enterprises—including those in tourism—remain in the analog space and are yet to modernize. The comparatively low uptake of new technologies by enterprises can in part be attributed to competitiveness deficits linked to the country's cumbersome business environment. Businesses in the Lao PDR, particularly those in tourism, remain disadvantaged by excessive licensing requirements and widespread informal practices. This regulatory setting has implications on enterprises' use of finance and technology, both of which are needed for improving service quality and market access to unlock firm growth. As a result, enterprise resilience to shocks remains weak, with an incomplete reform agenda affecting the productive potential and risk exposure of the private sector. A transformative reform agenda to address the country's deficits in tourism competitiveness is needed, including greater focus on business development across supply chains, investments, and the regulatory environment.

Source: ADB. 2022. *Southeast Asia Rising from the Pandemic*. Manila.

Trade in organic agricultural goods. Through the ADB-financed Sustainable Natural Resources and Productivity Enhancement Project and Smallholder Development Project, farmers sell their organically grown vegetables at That Luang market.

VIII
UPGRADING PATHS: REGIONAL INTEGRATION FOR EXPANDING GLOBAL TRADE

The emergence of GVCs offers faster and easier pathways to industrialization for many countries, including the Lao PDR, and participation and positioning in GVCs are important components of a development strategy for developing economies. The GVC concept involves breaking up the production process so that different production segments or tasks can be carried out in different countries where they can be performed most efficiently. These activities have increased significantly from 1990 onward, driven by lower trade costs—both natural and policy-related, as well as developments in information and communication technologies. In the context of regional integration, GVCs create possibilities for the development of complementary activities—upstream, midstream, downstream—in different countries within a region.[9]

Development of regional value chains and ensuring the connectedness of a region, such as the GMS, offers an avenue for obtaining greater benefits from global trade. Preferential regional trade agreements can be a potential important driver of such complementary activities. The Lao PDR has bilateral trade agreements with

---
[9] ADB. 2021. *The Greater Mekong Subregion 2030 and Beyond: Integration, Upgrading, Cities, and Connectivity*. Manila.

most GMS members. It is also party to several multilateral trade agreements, the latest of which is the Regional Comprehensive Economic Partnership—the world's largest trade deal that came into effect in 2022. This agreement includes specifications related to rules of origin, anti-dumping duties, technical barriers to trade, sanitary and phytosanitary standards, and procurement provision. As such, it offers an opportunity to action in important trade reforms. In addition, the partners with which the Lao PDR has already signed preferential trade agreements are already some of the most efficient and low-cost producers in the world. As such, the Lao PDR is unlikely to experience trade diversion from participation in such trade agreement, but rather experience only trade creation.[10] The Lao PDR's status of "least developed country" until 2026 allows it certain trade preferences associated with rules of origin provisions, along with waivers for the implementation of selected agreements of the World Trade Organization. With its graduation from least developed status looming, now is the time to prepare for transition.

Data from ADB's Asian Economic Integration Report 2021 shows that the participation of the Lao PDR in global and regional value chains has steadily increased over the last 2 decades (Figure 15).[11] Participation in global and regional value chains increased from 36% to 40% and 19% to 25% between 2000 and 2019, respectively. While the Lao PDR's involvement in global trade remains higher than in regional trade, the growth in participation of the Lao PDR in regional trade has been more rapid than in global trade. The degree of participation, however, is different from the position of a country in the value chain, with positioning more important for triggering structural transformation.

A country's position in a GVC has important implications for the benefits that it may be able to derive from the trade associated with its participation therein. For example, activities associated with product innovation, such as design and product development, tend to provide opportunities for high-wage employment, as do activities in post-production services, such as marketing. Activities in the middle

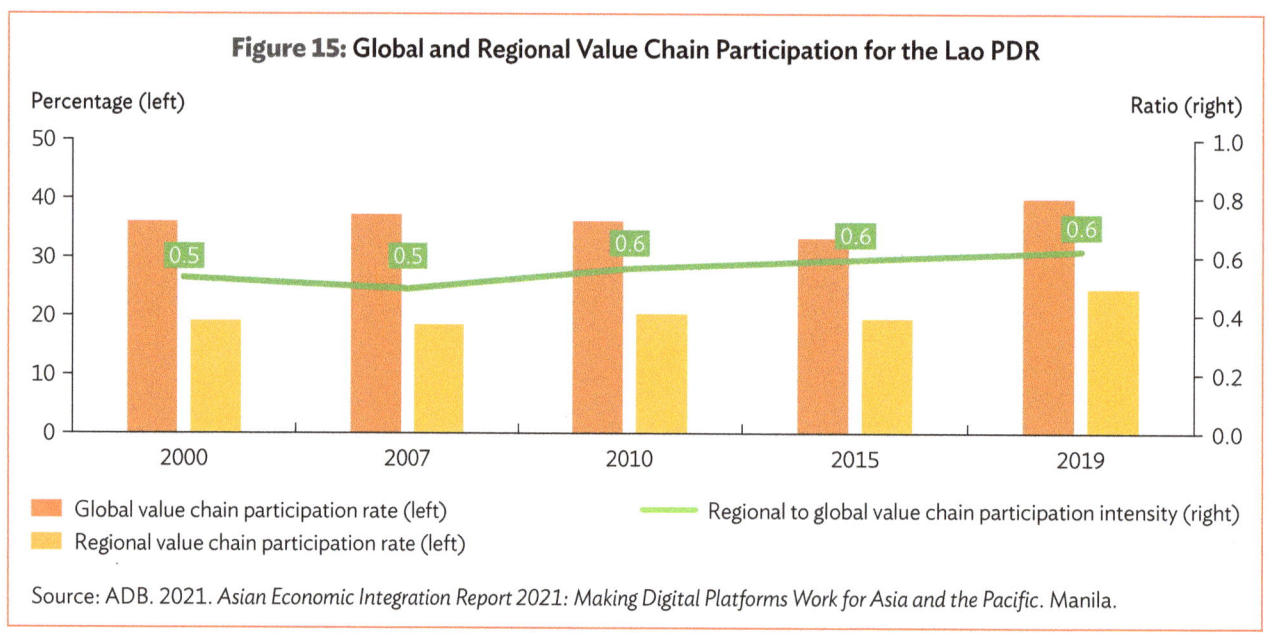

Figure 15: Global and Regional Value Chain Participation for the Lao PDR

Source: ADB. 2021. *Asian Economic Integration Report 2021: Making Digital Platforms Work for Asia and the Pacific*. Manila.

---

[10] ADB. 2021. *The Greater Mekong Subregion 2030 and Beyond: Integration, Upgrading, Cities, and Connectivity*. Manila.
[11] ADB. 2021. *Asian Economic Integration Report 2021: Making Digital Platforms Work for Asia and the Pacific*. Manila.

of the value chain, related to primary inputs, the production of intermediate goods, and final assembly, tend to capture a lower share of value and offer lower wages. Examination of the structure of imports and exports of countries can help to understand their positioning in a value chain. For the Lao PDR, the share of final goods in total imports is comparatively high, while the country's import of intermediate goods is comparatively low when contrasted with other GMS members (Figure 16). Primary intermediate goods, including raw materials, account for approximately half of goods exports, suggesting the importance of natural resource endowments in the country's trade (Figure 17). Mirroring this, export of processed consumption goods is comparatively low when contrasted with other GMS members.

The structure of goods trade of the Lao PDR highlights provisioning of primary inputs as an important contribution to its regional trade, and much of this trade takes place with other GMS members rather than other destinations in both regional and global markets. That is, the Lao PDR tends to be engaged in value chains "upstream," as a provider of raw materials and primary products for supporting the goods production processes for exporting activities in other GMS members. Such "upstream" positioning in value chains tends to be associated with relatively low wages. Over time, the Lao PDR should strategize to move to downstream positioning in the value chain, involving value addition and producing finished products for distribution and final consumption. Within value chains, these activities are typically associated with higher wages (Figure 18).

Moving downstream is not a straightforward process and will require investments to meet standards in food quality, health, and sanitation as well as environmental and climate impact, among others. In addition, it requires industry-specific analysis to better target decision-making. For example, making decisions about productivity-driven investments in plantations vis-à-vis value positioning in organic farming.

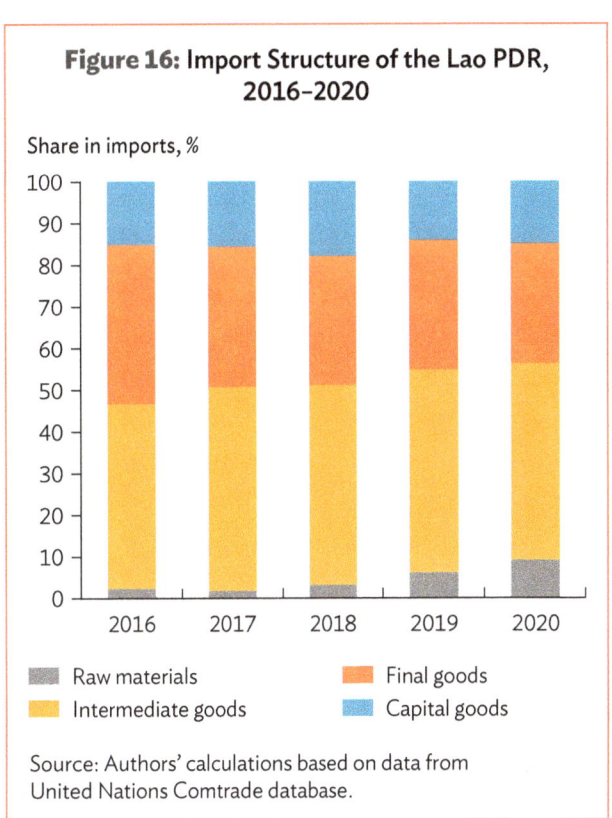

Figure 16: Import Structure of the Lao PDR, 2016–2020

Source: Authors' calculations based on data from United Nations Comtrade database.

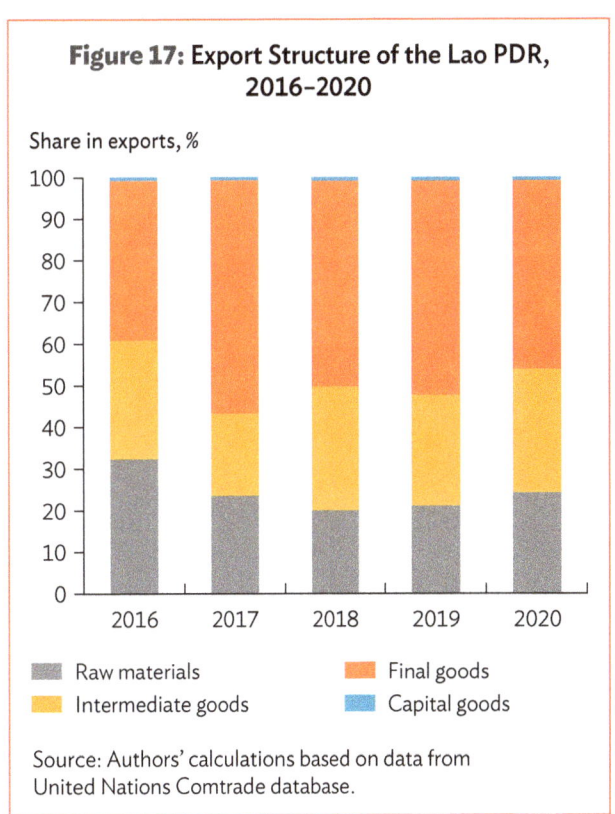

Figure 17: Export Structure of the Lao PDR, 2016–2020

Source: Authors' calculations based on data from United Nations Comtrade database.

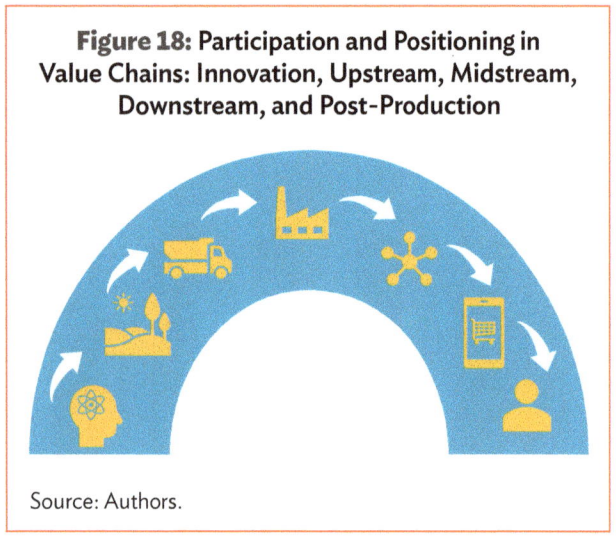

Figure 18: Participation and Positioning in Value Chains: Innovation, Upstream, Midstream, Downstream, and Post-Production

Source: Authors.

Policies and strategies should consider options to improve both participation and positioning in value chains. To this end, a two-pronged approach may be considered. First, seeking participation in value chains by taking advantage of comparative advantages, such as lower labor costs, and improving regulatory frameworks to minimize relocation and operating costs. Examples include those related to the time and cost of business registration and licensing as well as customs processing times and reliability of supply of electricity and internet services.

Analysis of the Lao PDR's manufacturing tariffs indicate that the country has a high share of zero tariff or low-rate tariffs, where the cost of tariff collection may outweigh the benefit from revenues raised.[12] Reassessing the role of these tariffs, with a view to reducing administrative and other opportunity costs, may help to improve business sentiment for attracting new investment. The number of nontariff measures increased to 520 in 2021 from 371 in 2015, with most measures acting as export restriction, technical barriers to trade, or quantity and price control measures, suggesting that they act as trade protection rather than product safety instruments.

Second is upgrading a country's position in both global and regional value chains. Economic upgrading in value chains consists of moving into higher value-added functions within the same chain or jumping into more technologically sophisticated value chains. Upgrading happens at the firm level, with macroeconomic stability, affordable credit, and quality education and training as workforce prerequisites for progress. It is also important that policy makers address information asymmetries, market failures, and path dependencies that result in underinvestment in upgrading by the private sector. More needs to be done to increase the number of large firms involved in manufacturing and value chains.

Improving participation and positioning in regional and global value chains is important for providing increased access to goods and services trade from the Lao PDR to markets beyond its borders. In addition, deepening integration in value chains may offer other benefits to the Lao PDR, such as access to information and encouraging technology transfer between firms at different stages of production in the value chain. This may then allow for greater mobility between upstream, midstream, and downstream positions within both regional and global value chains.

Entering into preferential trade agreements on exports together with the GMS members and economies in Southeast Asia is another important opportunity for expanding cooperation with GMS members, including leveraging benefits from knowledge transfers and development of shared production capabilities. This may help to maintain the country value chain participation and positioning, while also opening potential for exporting to more diverse trade partners.

---

[12] ADB. 2021. *The Greater Mekong Subregion 2030 and Beyond: Integration, Upgrading, Cities, and Connectivity*. Manila.

Vocational training. A plumbing student works at the main campus of the Champasak TVET Institution in Pakxe.

IX

THE FOURTH INDUSTRIAL REVOLUTION: IMPLICATIONS FOR THE LAO PDR AND THE GREATER MEKONG SUBREGION

New and emerging technologies are rapidly changing business processes across all sectors of the economy. Globally, the availability of new technologies and pace of change has accelerated since the onset of the COVID-19 pandemic, catalyzed by mobility restrictions imposed across nations which impacted the operations of industries and enterprises. A key feature observed in industry due to these policy dynamics is growing interconnection and complementarities between digital and physical production systems, with many manual tasks vulnerable to automation. These new technologies include robotics, artificial intelligence, the Internet of Things, and big data, among others.

There is concern that these new technologies may erode the competitive advantage of countries that have low wages and a large pool of unskilled workers, such as the Lao PDR. Concerns are particularly relevant in the context of regional trade and GVCs, as automation options provide alternatives to offshoring production to markets that have competitive advantages due to lower wage costs. At the same time, these technologies offer fresh opportunities to domestic firms, particularly through partnering with international firms, to improve productivity through technological adoption and benefit from related spillovers for competing on a regional and global scale.

Currently, the Lao PDR has a comparatively low level of trade and production associated with new technologies of the so-called Fourth Industrial Revolution, such as import and export of three-dimensional printing, computer-aided design and computer-aided manufacturing, and robotics. However, other countries are using this technology in sectors and products, such as agricultural crops, electronics, and textiles, where the Lao PDR may expand in future. Furthermore, the Lao PDR is a "follower" when it comes to both producing and using these new technologies. Being in this position entails more limited access to information, knowledge, and capabilities for obtaining comparative advantage in the production and the use of these new technologies. It also requires the updating of infrastructure, institutions, and human capital to realize potential. However, development of capacities in these new areas of production technology is an important avenue through which the Lao PDR may increase its participation in regional and global trade.

Technology and innovation continue to be an important driver of job creation and job destruction within and between sectors, as they have always been. However, with technology there will be opportunities for higher quality and higher-paid jobs that benefit the whole of the economy and society. In the post-COVID-19 world, the emphasis of investors may have shifted from lean production to holding inventory or recentralizing operations. They may be looking at vertical integration rather than relying on outsourcing. In this context, the quality of public institutions, including regulations, compliance, and legal certainty, is likely to weigh more heavily in the decision-making of investors' choice of location.

Policy will come to grips with these ongoing changes and play an important role in ensuring equitable structural change that involves moving into more complex activities that are associated with higher wages. This includes addressing issues of institutional weaknesses and deploying policies that encourage investment in higher education and training to develop more complex competencies and skills. Measures to enable flexible labor market transitions, particularly through social security system development, are needed for enterprises and workers.

Vientiane. This livable capital city supports the sharing of physical and institutional infrastructure for productivity-driven growth.

THE ROLE OF CITIES AS ENGINES OF GROWTH: AGGLOMERATION ECONOMIES

Urbanization plays a pivotal role in economic development, as this is where opportunities for agglomeration economies exist and where much of the structural transformation process takes place. The Lao PDR has experienced considerable urbanization since 1970, with approximately one-in-three people living in urban areas in 2020 (Figure 19). Urbanization has been driven by high average annual urban growth rates. Between 2000 and 2005, the urban growth rate high was 5.8%. However, between 2010 and 2020, it stabilized at a moderate growth rate, averaging 3.3% per annum (Figure 20). Urbanization is projected to progress steadily in the Lao PDR. Urban dwellers as a share of the population are expected to reach 47.7% by 2025.[13]

---

[13] Government of the Lao PDR. 2021. *Implementation of the 2030 Agenda for Sustainable Development (Voluntary National Review)*. Vientiane.

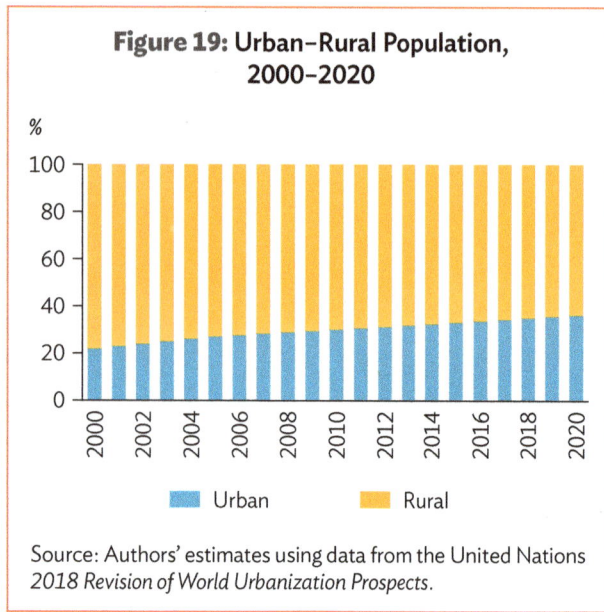

Figure 19: Urban–Rural Population, 2000–2020

Source: Authors' estimates using data from the United Nations *2018 Revision of World Urbanization Prospects*.

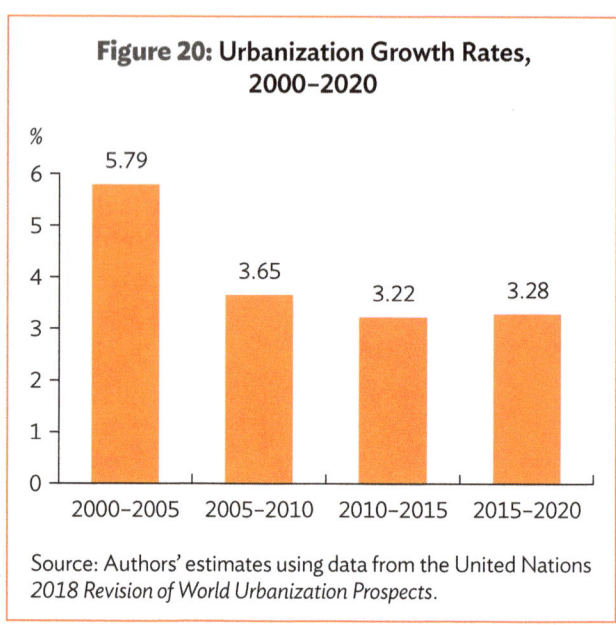

Figure 20: Urbanization Growth Rates, 2000–2020

Source: Authors' estimates using data from the United Nations *2018 Revision of World Urbanization Prospects*.

Although urbanization has proceeded at a faster pace in the Lao PDR over the last decade compared to the early period, the country's cities have remained relatively small, with most cities reported to have less than 300,000 inhabitants. Only Vientiane has grown substantially in terms of its number of inhabitants, from 0.4 million in 2000 to 1.4 million in 2020.[14]

Below Vientiane there are second-tier cities which are provincial capitals, namely Kaysone Phomvihane, Louangphabang, and Pakxe with populations close to 100,000 people. These cities were granted municipal status in 2018. Third tier towns are the remaining provincial capitals and smaller towns with populations of less than 30,000. Key towns and cities are located along National Road 13 (NR13), stretching from Vientiane to Luang Namtha (NR13 North) and from Vientiane to the Cambodia border (NR13 South), which parallels the Mekong river.

Measures of economic development and urbanization are typically closely related. But the trend of urbanization in the Lao PDR implies that it has been driven by the emergence of many small cities. This means the clustering of productive industries and resources is likely to be more limited.

Analysis of nighttime lights data confirms that the urbanization landscape in the Lao PDR is dominated by the capital city of Vientiane (Table 3). To illustrate, according to nighttime lights data, Vientiane accounts for 68% of the Lao PDR's urban population, followed by Kaysone Phomvihane at 9.9%, Pakxe at 10.3%, Louangphabang at 7.1%, and Thakhek at 4.7%. These four small cities that have populations ranging from 50,000 to 120,000 people. The remaining population live in towns with 50,000 people or less. This indicates that small cities and towns may have an untapped potential and could play a more important role in the urbanization process in the future. It also highlights a concern regarding spatial overconcentration of economic resources in the capital city and an associated risk of deepening spatial economic inequalities between the capital and other provinces in the country. Currently, public resources are allocated based on population size and domestic revenue collected by provinces and transferred to the central government.

---

[14] Figures covering both Vientiane capital and municipality. Lao Statistics Bureau. 2020. *Statistical Yearbook: 2020*. Vientiane.

Table 3: Nighttime Lights Data for the Lao PDR, 2000 and 2016

	2000	2020
Urban population (million)	0.4	1.1
City size:		
• 0.5 million–1 million (%)	0.0	68.0 (Vientiane)
• 0.3 million–0.5 million (%)	81.7 (Vientiane)	0.0
• <0.3 million (%)	18.3[a]	32.0[b]
Total (%)	100.0	100.0

[a] Kaysone Phomvihane, Louangphabang.
[b] Kaysone Phomvihane, Louangphabang, Pakxe, Thakhek.

Source: ADB's estimates using nighttime lights images from the Defense Meteorological Satellite Program and Visible Infrared Imaging Radiometer Suite of the National Oceanic and Atmospheric Administration and grid population data from LandScan Data sets of the Oak Ridge National.

As such, current arrangements mean that cities will receive resources depending on economic activity and the associated government revenues. To mitigate the risk of deepening spatial economic inequalities, the Lao PDR will need to successfully develop its small cities to medium-sized and large cities, while ensuring allocation of resources equally across populations in urban and rural areas to avoid "big city" bias.

A comparison of the administrative border of Vientiane capital and municipality with the natural border of the city using nighttime lights images indicates that there is great scope for expanding spatially within the administrative boundaries of the city. For Vientiane capital and municipality, the administrative area was estimated at 3,600 square kilometers (km^2), while the natural city border area was estimated at 800 km^2 in 2020. This suggests that there is a vast amount of room for further urban expansion within the existing administrative borders of the capital, although it is important that care is given to minimizing "big city" bias. At the same time, this also means that there are considerable volumes of rural land in the same area.

This entails an administratively complex situation for the authorities. Rather than just functioning as managers of cities, the governments of Vientiane capital and municipality would need to support rural and urban development and adopt policies to strike a balance between rural and urban priorities within their jurisdiction.

For the Lao PDR and the broader GMS area, the evidence shows that firms are more likely to innovate products and processes and invest in research and development when located in larger cities. This suggests a strong link between growth in urbanization and productivity. However, in the Lao PDR, the link between urban expansion and the economy has been weaker than what has been observed in other countries in developing Asia. This may be due to the small size of cities as well as the country's resource-dependent growth model. Furthermore, the low quality of institutions and weak governance may have limited the country's potential to leverage from agglomeration economies for using its cities as engines of growth.[15]

---

[15] ADB. 2020. *Report on the 2020 Country Performance Assessment Exercise*. Manila.

This points to an urgent need for strategies that can help the country reap the full benefit of the urbanization process. Without such focus, the process of economic diversification for structural transformation is likely to continue to lag. For example, many small towns in the Lao PDR are in the border areas of the country. Identifying ways to leverage locational benefits, such as cross-border city partnership agreements, may be one strategy for accelerating development progress. Focus on how to build cities deserves the attention of policy makers because cities can drive increases in productivity through benefits known as "agglomeration economies." Figure 21 explains that the benefits of agglomeration economies are primarily derived through three main mechanisms: matching, learning, and sharing. First, large and dense cities allow a more efficient **matching** between inputs and outputs. Second, as individuals and organizations interact, knowledge spillovers are more likely to take place and result in **learning** that leads to innovation. Third, cities enable greater **sharing** of physical and institutional infrastructure, as well as niche resources, for greater efficiency. Improvements in matching, learning, and sharing are essential for productivity-driven growth.

The benefits of economies of agglomeration arise from urbanization processes taking place. They thrive on increasing rates of return because of low costs and increased productivity from low transportation costs, geographic advantages, labor pooling and matching, and knowledge spillovers. Meanwhile, areas designated as special economic zones (SEZs) also seek to boost economic activity and job creation, but they are typically established in border areas or gateways to international markets. Since the first SEZ was established in 2003, much of the foreign investment in manufacturing has been channeled through these areas. There are currently 12 SEZs operating in the country. Many more are proposed, but often these proposals lack sound urban development master plans. However, these zones apply business and trade regulations differently from the rest of the country, with firms in these areas benefiting from a set of specific

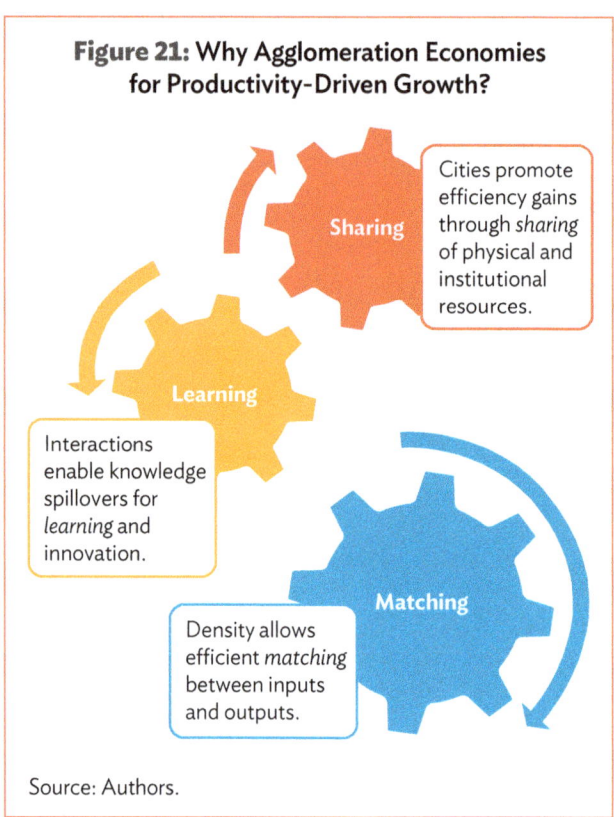

Figure 21: Why Agglomeration Economies for Productivity-Driven Growth?

Sharing — Cities promote efficiency gains through *sharing* of physical and institutional resources.

Learning — Interactions enable knowledge spillovers for *learning* and innovation.

Matching — Density allows efficient *matching* between inputs and outputs.

Source: Authors.

investment, tax, labor, and other incentive policies that provide cost advantages for being globally competitive. SEZs therefore tend to behave in different ways to urban areas, and their associated benefits are also different, particularly concerning their implications for equitable and inclusive growth.

Figure 22 summarizes policies to support agglomeration economies, illustrating how to ensure that urbanization can play a stronger role as an engine of growth. It highlights the importance of (i) investing in urban infrastructure, such as city transport systems, water and sanitation systems, labor market institutions, and affordable housing; and (ii) ensuring a supportive business environment, with policies providing a regulatory framework that fosters cities as good places to do business, innovate, and accumulate human capital. This includes quality infrastructure for industry development, especially that which promotes productivity-driven manufacturing growth such as industrial parks and market connectivity.

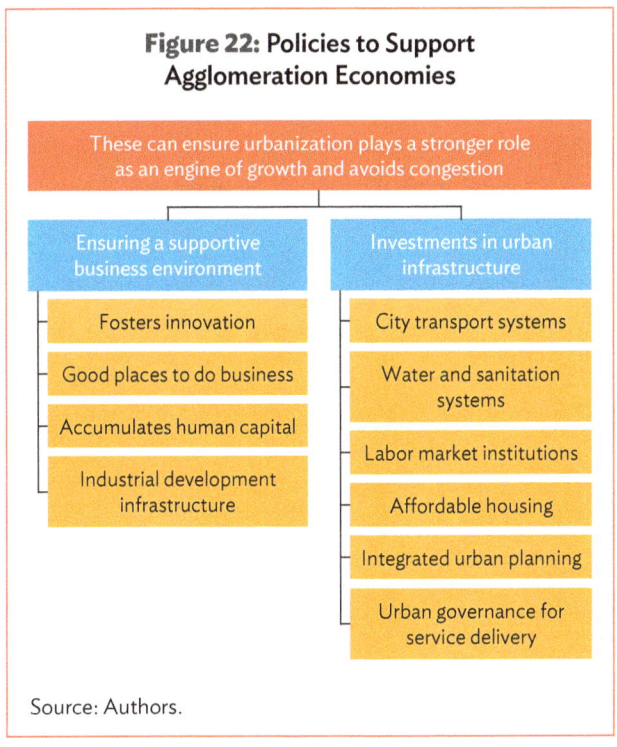

Figure 22: Policies to Support Agglomeration Economies

Source: Authors.

Urban infrastructure and services investments are critical for enabling the functioning of cities and ensuring that they do not get overwhelmed by the forces of congestion including pollution, and environmental degradation, among others. Traffic congestion in Vientiane is swelling, pollution is building up, and road accidents are on the rise—imposing limitations on the city's potential as an engine of sustainable growth.[16] Traffic congestion results from the inability of the supply of transport infrastructure to keep up with traffic demand. Developing the public transport system is critical. Inadequate transport infrastructure exacerbates another fundamental issue for urbanization: access to adequate and affordable housing. In the Lao PDR, demand for urban housing has continuously exceeded supply, leading to a rapid increase in urban housing prices. The price-to-income ratios of house prices to annual household incomes are estimated at 23 in the Lao PDR, meaning it takes 23 times an average household's annual income to own a home in the medium-sized city of Vientiane.[17] As a result of comparatively high housing prices, many still live in inadequate housing or informal slum settlements and lack access to clean water and sanitation infrastructure.

In addition to urban infrastructure, intercity and regional infrastructure is requisite to accommodate industries along economic corridors. For example, to deliver finished precision machinery in good condition to its destination on time, it is necessary to have good quality roads that are free from vibration. Furthermore, integrated urban planning and urban governance for service delivery offer strategies to realize economic potential in urban agglomeration and minimize adverse social, environmental, and climate change impacts. In urban areas, commerce, social necessities, and environmental concerns compete for finite land supply. Improved mobility through planning of transit-oriented development and multimodal integration helps realize urban economic potential by connecting people to jobs and educational opportunities.

Urban planning quality has implications for the trajectory of a city's development. It influences the extent to which congestion may take hold. Progress on the implementation of the 2011 Vientiane Urban Master Plan needs to be expedited. With urbanization expected to continue at a rapid pace, policy makers must strengthen the capacity of their urban planners to adequately respond. This includes identifying potential development corridors, preparing the associated master plans for these areas, and acquiring land rights for transport grids, public facilities, and open spaces before development commences. In addition, social issues such as availability of health services need to be addressed. One approach is through the GMS health cooperation strategy (Box 6).

---

[16] ADB. 2021. *Lao PDR: Setting Vientiane on the Road to Sustainable Transport*. Manila.
[17] ADB. 2021. *The Greater Mekong Subregion 2030 and Beyond: Integration, Upgrading, Cities, and Connectivity*. Manila.

Box 6: Greater Mekong Subregion Health Cooperation Strategy, 2019–2023

With increasing regional integration, the risk of cross-border spread of emerging, reemerging, and epidemic-prone diseases also rises. High variance in the quality of health care systems and social safety net programs also poses a major challenge, particularly for labor mobility and border security. The Lao People's Democratic Republic, for example, will need sustained investment in health systems strengthening to enable it to realize a full range of potential benefits of regional integration. The Greater Mekong Subregion (GMS) Health Cooperation Strategy 2019–2023 presents a framework to guide the GMS countries in their efforts to address health issues affecting the subregion. The table below presents the pillars of the strategy, its programming priorities, crosscutting issues, and enablers to support improvements on health performance.

GMS Health Cooperation Strategic Framework

Strategic Pillars		
1. Health security as a regional public good	2. Health impacts of connectivity and mobility	3. Health workforce development
Programming Areas		
• Core IHR capacities of national health systems	• Border area health system strengthening	• Regional health cooperation leadership
• One Health response to public health threats	• UHC for migrant and mobile populations	• Intraregional capacity building
• Cross-border and subregional cooperation on health security	• Health impact assessment of GMS urban and transport infrastructure development	
Crosscutting		
Policy convergence — Gender mainstreaming — Inclusive and equitable development		
Enablers		
Synergies between regional plans and programs	Stakeholder engagement	Research and knowledge products	Information and communication technology	Cross-sector cooperation and coordination

GMS = Greater Mekong Subregion, IHR = international health regulations, UHC = universal health care.

Source: ADB. 2019. *Greater Mekong Subregion Health Cooperation Strategy 2019–2023*. Manila.

Some cities and towns experience urbanization more rapidly than others given their geography, access to transportation networks, and economic base. Vientiane will continue to be the country's dominant and primary city. With increased migration, density, and concentration of economic activities, actions will be needed to address urban sprawl, housing shortages, and traffic congestion, as these issues will intensify in the future. The cities and towns located along NR13, the Lao PDR's main transport backbone, are expected to experience continued growth well into the future, given their accessibility and proximity to the neighboring countries of Thailand and Viet Nam. Towns in northern parts of the country that are less accessible are expected to experience slower growth than other provincial capitals. Given foreign investments in agricultural production in these areas, there is potential for future growth for high-value crop farming and ecotourism.

National and subnational governments can support agglomeration economies by addressing the concerns of private enterprises on the business environment through policy reforms and ensuring their effective and transparent implementation. Results of enterprise surveys on provincial trade facilitation show that policy reforms that consolidated regulatory requirements on enterprises reduced the cost of business registration (Table 4). However, the same surveys also found that there was lack of meaningful progress on transparency and access to information, and companies in the Lao PDR remain disadvantaged by excessive licensing requirements and informal practices. Figure 23 presents further information on the obstacles that firms perceive they encounter in doing business. Access to markets, followed by the quality of regulatory environment, are the most frequently identified problems for firms in the Lao PDR, although the latter has improved in recent years. Electricity access, arguably the single most critical infrastructure for modern production, is an obstacle that places limitations on the operations of 14.4% of firms. Combined, the obstacles faced by businesses limit their ability to realize their aspirations to compete at regional and global levels, with substantial progress in terms of improving the business environment required.

Table 4: Provincial Trade Facilitation Index, 2017 and 2019

Index	2019	2017	Change
Overall	**55.4**	**48.8**	**6.6**
Starting a business	67.0	59.0	8.0
Transparency and access to information	26.9	40.8	(13.9)
Regulatory burden	74.7	59.0	15.7
Informal charges	50.1	46.1	4.0
Consistency in implementation	53.9	37.7	16.2
Business friendliness	59.6	60.2	(0.6)

( ) = negative.
Note: 100 is best and 0 is worst.
Source: ADB. 2022. *Provincial Facilitation for Investment and Trade Index: Measuring Economic Governance for Business Development in the Lao People's Democratic Republic—Second Edition.* Manila.

The concentration of people and resources in cities opens opportunities for matching, learning, and sharing to take place that leads to agglomeration economies, making cities engines of growth. However, such benefits can be overshadowed by congestion and the quality of the regulatory environment.

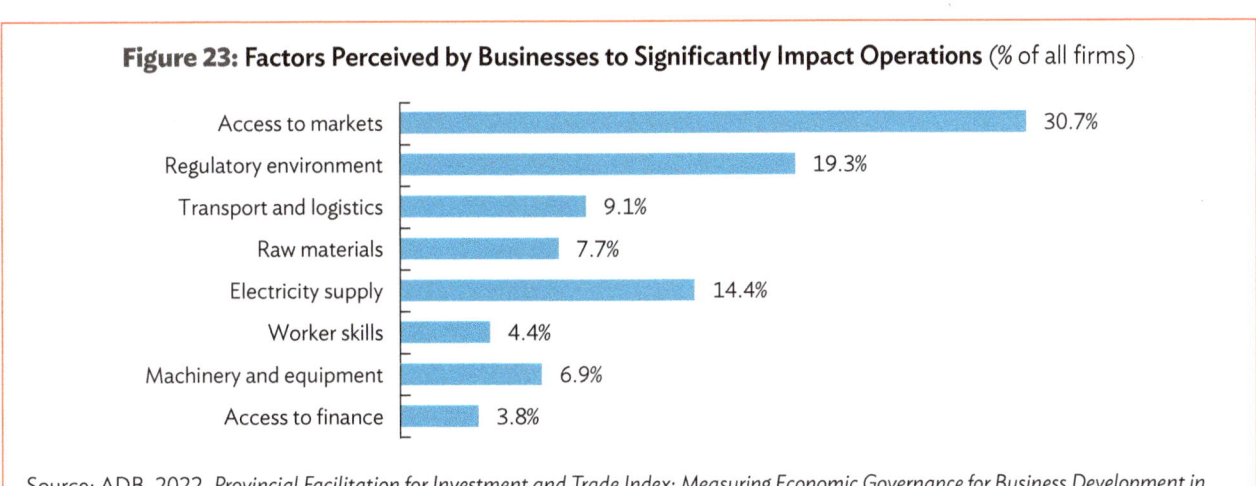

Figure 23: Factors Perceived by Businesses to Significantly Impact Operations (% of all firms)

- Access to markets: 30.7%
- Regulatory environment: 19.3%
- Transport and logistics: 9.1%
- Raw materials: 7.7%
- Electricity supply: 14.4%
- Worker skills: 4.4%
- Machinery and equipment: 6.9%
- Access to finance: 3.8%

Source: ADB. 2022. *Provincial Facilitation for Investment and Trade Index: Measuring Economic Governance for Business Development in the Lao People's Democratic Republic—Second Edition.* Manila.

As a guiding principle, managing the tension between agglomeration and congestion requires that cities have sufficient investment in core infrastructure such as transport, water, and sanitation, as well as regulations that facilitate residents to conduct their business with ease. These fundamental hard and soft infrastructures are ideally embedded within a milieu conducive to sustained product and process innovations through investments in human capital and friendly business environments.[18] Without sufficient planning and building controls, urban development will occur through sprawl. This is already evident in Vientiane, Kaysone Phomvihane, and Pakxe. Louangphabang has been able to avoid this because of strict controls within the core/heritage area; however rapid development is likely to occur beyond this area.

Cities do not exist in isolation, rather they are connected to one another as well as to rural areas, through flow of goods, services, and people. For example, small towns play a key role in ensuring that the food supply chain functions efficiently by linking farmers and their produce to consumers in the city. Economic functions and activities of one area often complement those of other areas, to make a "system." This system is enabled through connectivity that is provided by the transport network, with the Government of the Lao PDR investing in several flagship initiatives over the last decade that have transformed the country from landlocked to "land-linked" (Box 6).

---

[18] ADB. 2021. *The Greater Mekong Subregion 2030 and Beyond: Integration, Upgrading, Cities, and Connectivity*. Manila.

Lao PDR–Viet Nam border. The border is located on the GMS East–West Economic Corridor or Route 9 linking Viet Nam to the Lao PDR and Thailand.

XI

CONNECTIVITY TO ENHANCE TRADE AND INTEGRATION IN THE LAO PDR AND THE GREATER MEKONG SUBREGION

The major goal of the GMS Program is to assist its members, including the Lao PDR, to drive forward economic growth through cross-border subregional connectivity and enhanced trade and investment. Development of economic corridors plays a critical role, as does the country's strategy of serving as a land bridge within the GMS through infrastructure investment, border agreements, and measures to improve cross-border logistics.

Economic corridor development typically starts with development of transport links in a specific geographic area based on economic potential and then expands into other types of infrastructure and capability investments. That is, an economic corridor often starts out as a transport corridor and then transforms into a multimodal transport corridor with road, rail, waterway, and air transport. This enables development of a logistics corridor and provides the basis for economic corridor development. Economic corridors must possess the following characteristics: (i) create links to major markets, (ii) have nodal points for centers of enterprise development, (iii) open up new investment opportunities, (iv) promote synergies through the clustering of projects, and (v) provide demonstration effects. As such, focus on economic corridor development, including better connectivity and logistics, supports export diversification and is an integral part of the GMS Program.

Connectivity in the Lao PDR is challenged due to its mountainous landscape and associated difficulties in building direct road routes. The ratios of road distance to straight-line distance in the districts of the Lao PDR are relatively higher than what is observed in other GMS countries, with connectivity worse in the mountainous northern parts of the country. Total road distance is at least twice the total of the shortest direct distances in many northern districts. There are also significant gaps between the better-connected western parts of the country and the worse-connected eastern parts. The average speed traveled in the country is approximately 50 kilometers per hour (Table 5). On average it takes 9 hours from the country's 139 districts to reach the capital, with the maximum travel time reaching 20 hours from some districts in the Lao PDR to Vientiane, even though they may be only a few hundred kilometers away by straight-line distance. Besides its mountainous landscape, weather also threatens the roads' integrity and connectivity. Roads are severely impacted by numerous landslides caused by catastrophic rains during the raining season.

Since cross-border trade and investment is one of the expected major engines of growth in the GMS Program, connectivity of districts to the main economic corridors that link to other members' capitals is important.

Table 5: Travel Time, Distance, and Average Speed to Vientiane from Districts in the Lao PDR

To the capital (overall rating)	Poor
Average duration (h)	9.32
Minimum duration (h)	0.38
Maximum duration (h)	20.16
Average distance (km)	472.26
Minimum distance (km)	10.18
Maximum distance (km)	913.98
Average speed (km/h)	50.67

h = hour, km = kilometer.
Note: Rating is based on average speed: up to 60 km/h = poor, 61–70 km/h = fair, and 71 km/h and above = good.
Source: Authors' calculations based on Open Source Routing Machine and database of global administrative boundaries.

The presence of the GMS economic corridors, North–South, Central, East–West, and Southern corridors help foster cross-border trade and investment as they give the districts along and nearby the corridors access to markets in all other five GMS countries bordering the Lao PDR. Table 6 shows the average time needed to reach Vientiane from all districts for each GMS member.

Table 6: Average Time Needed to Reach Vientiane from Greater Mekong Subregion Capitals (hours)

From Districts in GMS Members	To Vientiane	To GMS Capitals	From Districts in the Lao PDR
Cambodia	14.59	Phnom Penh	19.39
Lao PDR	9.32	Yangon	22.48
Myanmar	25.44	Bangkok	14.28
Thailand	9.69	Ha Noi	15.72
Viet Nam	17.88	Ho Chi Minh City	22.04
(PRC) Guangxi	21.87	Nanning	21.11
(PRC) Yunnan	26.08	Kunming	22.23

GMS = Greater Mekong Subregion, Lao PDR = Lao People's Democratic Republic, PRC = People's Republic of China.
Source: Authors' calculations based on Open-Source Routing Machine and database of global administrative boundaries.

It takes districts in the Lao PDR 9 hours on average to reach the capital Vientiane, while the same districts take 14 hours to Bangkok, Thailand, or 16 hours to reach Ha Noi, Viet Nam. Given the difference in market size of capital cities in other GMS countries, it is understandable that districts along the border in the Lao PDR may focus their efforts on cross-border trade rather than on trade with their own capital city.

Better access to larger markets in the GMS would bring about opportunities for higher economic growth in the Lao PDR. The most efficient way to increase access to larger markets in the GMS is to improve connectivity with their large cities. With improved connectivity to large cities in the GMS, it is possible to leverage benefits from existing infrastructure to reduce the time to access other cities. This may then encourage investments in logistics infrastructure and improve a country's trade prospects. However, the Lao PDR's performance on logistics indexes points to broader challenges that need to be addressed to improve trade within and outside the GMS, including aspects related to the efficiency of clearance processes, timeliness, and tracking and tracing (Figure 24).[19] Cargo reaching its destination within an expected delivery schedule stands out as a particular challenge. This represents a serious risk to trade businesses and a threat to deepening engagement with GVCs. For example, limited refrigerated transport or cold storage, coupled with longer than expected travel times, imply heightened risks associated with loss of produce.

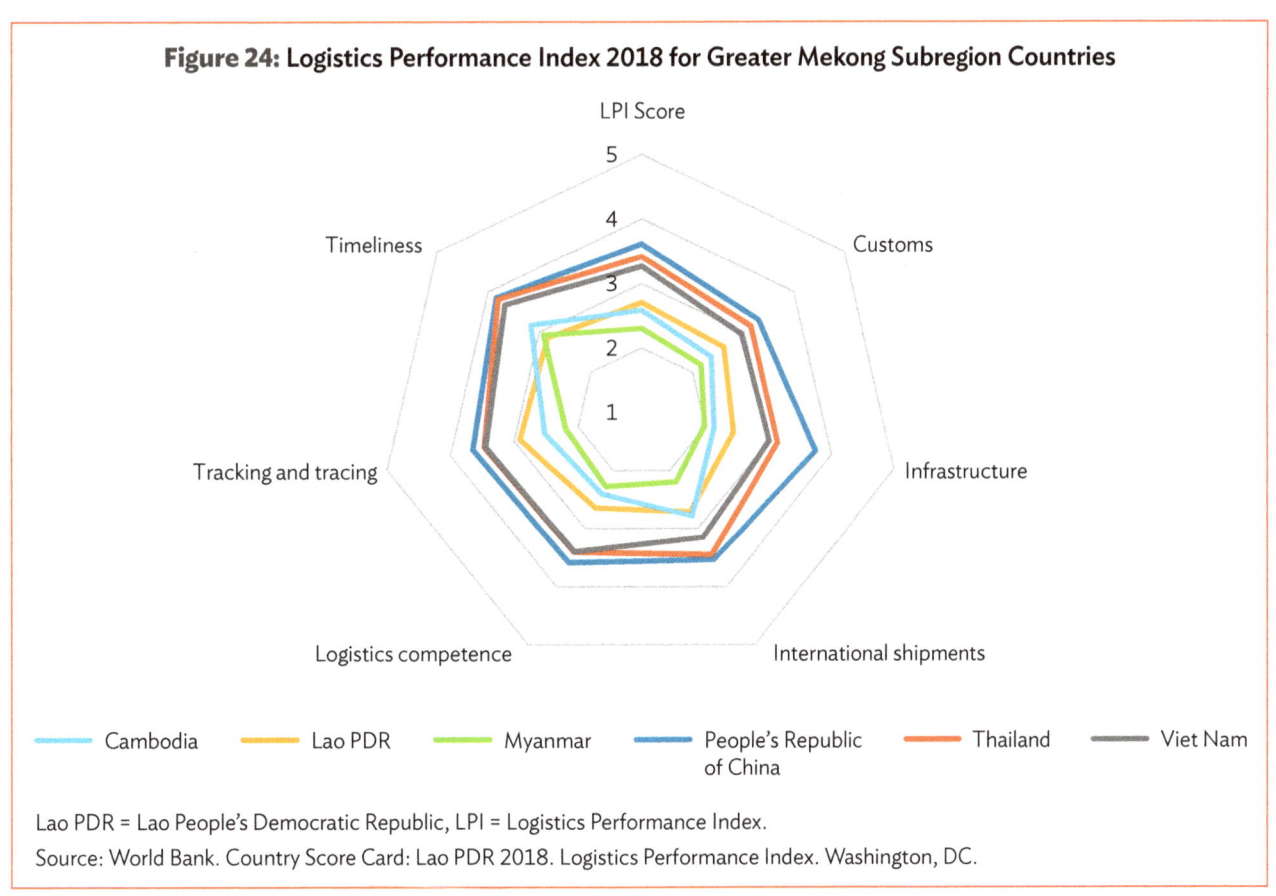

Figure 24: Logistics Performance Index 2018 for Greater Mekong Subregion Countries

Lao PDR = Lao People's Democratic Republic, LPI = Logistics Performance Index.
Source: World Bank. Country Score Card: Lao PDR 2018. Logistics Performance Index. Washington, DC.

---

[19] World Bank. Country Score Card: Lao PDR 2018. Logistics Performance Index. Washington, DC.

> **Box 7: Landlocked to Land-Linked in the Lao PDR: 2010–2021 Achievements and 2030 Targets**
>
> The Lao People's Democratic Republic (Lao PDR) has made significant progress in developing road and rail network infrastructure between 2011 and 2021. The country invested significant financial resources in building bridges, highways, and railways connecting with neighboring countries to support the expansion of regional trade, investment, and tourism. The most outstanding achievements during this period were completion of the Vientiane–Vang Vieng Highway on 2 December 2020 and the Lao PDR–People's Republic of China (PRC) Railway on 3 December 2021. These two mega projects have been a showcase in connecting the Lao PDR with the PRC. Current investments in rail and road under the Belt and Road Initiative amount to $7 billion, or 40% of the Lao PDR's gross domestic product, a proportionally much larger investment than is the case for any of its Southeast Asian peers.
>
> In its Ninth National Socio-Economic Development Plan, the Government of the Lao PDR aims to deepen economic diversification and regional integration through measures to transform the country from a landlocked to a land-linked country, leveraging its strategic location to partake in the Asian growth. It plans to build, upgrade, rehabilitate, and maintain 2,800 kilometers of land transport infrastructure, including roads, bridges, and highways as part of the network along the economic corridors connecting with the neighboring countries. It will also undertake a feasibility study, survey and design, construction and maintenance of the expressway, railways, and railway facilities including the Ha Noi–Vientiane, Vientiane–Boten and Vientiane–Champasak Highways.
>
> The Lao PDR and Viet Nam are exploring multimodal cross-border transportation projects, including a railway that runs from the Lao PDR's Vientiane capital to Vung Ang seaport of Viet Nam's central Ha Tinh province and an expressway linking Viet Nam's Ha Noi and Vientiane capital. The various transportation modes will help the Lao PDR to realize its vision of becoming a regional logistics hub that will boost regional trade and the economy.
>
> Transport infrastructure plays perhaps the most central role in facilitating and sustaining mutually beneficial relationships among key locations within an economy in GMS members. The key production centers have been connected by major road networks.
>
> Sources: Government of the Lao PDR. 2021. *Ninth National Socio-Economic Development Plan*. Vientiane; ADB. 2021. *The Greater Mekong Subregion 2030 and Beyond: Integration, Upgrading, Cities, and Connectivity*. Manila.

The government is proactively addressing these issues, including plans to improve connectivity with Viet Nam through an economic corridor development initiative (Box 7). Substantial progress in connectivity has already been made through the completion of flagship infrastructure projects, including the Vientiane–Vang Vieng Highway in 2020 and the Lao PDR–PRC Railway in 2021. The development of the Lao PDR–PRC Railway is expected to reduce transport and logistics costs by as much as 40%.[20] In addition, these investments open opportunity for more cross-border transit trade in the Lao PDR. A key issue is to ensure that these infrastructure investments provide benefits to communities and local businesses, particularly through improved market access to GMS and other global markets. This will require policies and investment to enhance logistics and competition, inclusive of business environment improvement measures and investments in connectivity and trade facilitation to reduce costs and delays at the border. After these major investments in connectivity infrastructure, it is important to ensure sufficient routine budget allocation for operation and maintenance of these facilities to ensure that the benefits of these assets accrue in the medium- to long-term.

---

[20] World Bank. 2020. *From Landlocked to Land-Linked: Unlocking the Potential of Lao-China Rail Connectivity*. Vientiane: The World Bank Group.

Women's empowerment. Thong Keumanvinong, 39, is a member of a cattle grazing group that received support under ADB's Smallholder Development Project. The project helped farming families in 19 villages adopt modern cattle grazing techniques that have improved the health of their animals and increased family incomes.

XII RECOMMENDATIONS

The Lao PDR's economy has experienced comparatively high rates of economic growth since the inception of the GMS economic cooperation program in 1992. However, its income levels are yet to converge with other countries in the GMS. Convergence in per capita incomes within the GMS will require the Lao PDR to grow substantially faster than other members in the coming decades. Strategies to diversify the economy through successfully leveraging the benefits of the country's strategic position are needed. To support progress in the coming decades, it will be important for economic policy to focus on the following three interrelated areas:

(i)   Deepening integration with the regional and global economy, including upgrading value chain positioning, adopting new technologies, and increasing production complexity.
(ii) Enabling cities to be engines of growth through fostering agglomeration economies.
(iii) Improving connectivity to enhance trade and integration in the Lao PDR and GMS.

The hope is that progress in these policy areas will contribute to achieving the twin objective of increasing the growth and convergence of the Lao PDR's economy within the GMS and with the world's leading economies.

Regional cooperation can be used as a powerful development escalator if coupled with a sound development strategy. There is an opportunity for the Lao PDR to advance its economy through trading with advanced economies as this opens opportunities to use its current comparative advantage to pursue upgrading strategies. Potential quick-win solutions targeted at resilient economic recovery and longer-term strategic directions for strengthening trade facilitation and investment outcomes are provided in Box 8.

The Lao PDR's economy still relies on a comparatively narrow set of goods to support its growth. However, the country's geographic location is a great asset that can be further leveraged. Regional integration therefore offers an important avenue for supporting the country's diversification efforts, with deepening cooperation with GMS members providing a source of opportunity for developing capabilities that support diversification efforts for opening access to more markets. Improving trade with regional markets can provide a pathway for diversification and upgrading, which may strengthen integration with global markets. While many approaches to diversification exist, trade and investment policies are often at the center of such efforts. Policies to support diversification and upgrading efforts include:

(i) strengthening trade and investment systems for evidence-based policy development,
(ii) reforming the investment climate to improve the business environment,
(iii) designing trade policies to encourage competition in markets,
(iv) facilitating trade to improve logistics and lower tariff and nontariff barriers,
(v) using export and investment promotion agencies, and
(vi) developing and implementing policies and plans to promote economic corridors.

Box 8: Enhancing Collaboration in Trade and Investment under the Greater Mekong Subregion Program

To preserve the gains of economic integration achieved over the past 3 decades, the Greater Mekong Subregion Program needs to respond to its members' needs by formulating "quick-win" solutions targeted at pandemic recovery while continuing to promote longer-term strategic development. The table summarizes potential interventions in the short-term and medium- to long-term.

Strengthening Trade and Investment Facilitation Capabilities

Quick Wins	Strategic Directions
(i) **Digitalization:** Equip local businesses with digital skills to remain competitive and bolster investment in digital infrastructure for greater digital connectivity.	(i) **Regional trade:** Implement the Regional Comprehensive Economic Partnership to bolster trade and investment policies and opportunities.
(ii) **Business environment:** Enhance one-stop services and tap existing platforms to improve access to information.	(ii) **SME development:** Improve business development services for enterprises, including access to finance for trade for both women and men and establish virtual marketplaces for exporters.
(iii) **Policy to optimize trade:** Prepare policies, guidelines, and regulations, including building capacity and technical expertise for implementation of free trade agreements.	(iii) **Enhance partnerships:** Strengthen intraregional cooperation by sharing best practices and strengthening engagement with regional cooperation platforms.
(iv) **Trade and investment taskforce:** An institutional mechanism to monitor progress for staying on track.	

SME = small and medium-sized enterprise.
Source: ADB. 2022. Scoping Study: Enhancing Collaboration in Trade and Investment under the GMS Program. Draft manuscript.

In refining a strategy for upgrading production structures, it is important to understand financing needs and the role of private investment therein, with policies designed to enable domestic and foreign investment inflows to meet such needs. Specific policies will be needed that target all production factors, including in areas of human capital development and entrepreneurship for both women and men. Export promotion, investment in knowledge, and technology upgrading are also key areas for policy attention. Moving ahead requires an environment that encourages firms to license foreign technology, train their workforce, and create linkages with local and foreign knowledge institutions. Workplaces will also need to comply with core international labor, environment, and governance standards, especially if they are to development long-term relationships with global investors.

Increasing participation in value chains requires encouraging inward foreign investment that attracts large multinational corporations, including through developing preferential trade agreements with other GMS members where significant trade potential exists. Investments in knowledge, capabilities, and technology may also support a movement toward greater downstream engagement in value chains. This includes investments that support uptake of the latest technologies associated with the Fourth Industrial Revolution, which requires a workforce with the requisite skills to develop, produce, and use these technologies. At the micro level, governments can play a role in linking enterprises with value chains through promoting industry and trade associations, strengthening the ecosystem of business development services, and ensuring consistency with the standards, certification, and accreditation with international norms.

Given that much of the Lao PDR's positioning in value chains is focused on upstream activity (e.g., raw materials and primary products), policies such as export taxes on raw materials may be useful to support downstream production. Applied sensibly and effectively, such policies can help steer greater downstream positioning in value chains. There are opportunities including optimizing the utilization of benefits under trade agreements that have been signed, including the recent Regional Comprehensive Economic Partnership. To further unlock the benefits of trade integration, the quality of coordination among various ministries needs to be improved.

For developing more diverse and more sophisticated products and services where there is potential for export, it is important to engage routinely in public–private dialogue. The Lao PDR organizes a Lao Business Forum annually. Public–private dialogues for promoting structural transformation can build on this mechanism while being as specific as possible. Focus should be given to identified products in agriculture and manufacturing, with a view to better understanding the constraints that the private sector faces in developing these products and, what, if any, is the role of the public sector in addressing these constraints. This dialogue should include the understanding of actual positioning of selected products and services in regional and global value chains, as well as how selected policy interventions may help to improve potential positioning. The objective of such dialogues is to obtain greater clarity on what is needed to support progress and the potential value that such investments in diversification and upgrading may offer for economic growth. These investigations will require further assessments and high-level commitment.

Cities tend to have high levels of productivity as they are more efficient at matching between inputs and outputs, fostering learning and innovation, and sharing resources. Hence, they can be an important engine of growth for the GMS, but they are vulnerable to congestion. Traffic congestion, weak urban planning, and a lack of affordable housing can offset the productivity advantages of cities. Therefore, ensuring an efficient and affordable multimodal transport system, expanding the supply of affordable housing, and investing in urban planning are important considerations in laying the foundation for quality urban development. The Lao PDR has already taken important steps in this direction by, for example, investing in development of a bus rapid transit system in Vientiane capital.

Beyond this, cities need to have conducive environments for the incubation and operations of new and dynamic firms. In practice, this means paying attention to institutions that build human capital, providing conducive business environments, and formulating policies to encourage new economic activities and young firms to operate. It is important that the government continue with a robust program of reform to allow a flourishing and vibrant private sector, inclusive of measures to ease business entry, enhance trade facilitation, and modernize sanitary and phytosanitary regulations, among others.

Cities of all sizes—small, medium-sized, and large—are important. For the Lao PDR it will be important to strategize on how to grow small cities into medium-sized cities. Some cities may benefit from improved connectivity with larger cities, and therefore grow, while other cities may experience declines in some lines of business activity as they become more connected. To address this issue, it is important for policy makers to find out why a city is lagging, that is, understand constraints to improving **matching**, **sharing**, and **learning**, and respond accordingly.

In addition, a general rule is that it is important to invest in human capital in a spatially neutral manner to promote inclusive development and reduce potential for emergence of spatial inequalities. This means ensuring access to good quality education and health care in small and remote cities, as much as those of large well-connected cities. A healthy and well-educated population is essential to unlocking potential and accelerating economic diversification processes.

In terms of connectivity and network development, road development is a priority for reducing travel times while trade facilitation requires investment across all components to allow for greater ease of matching, sharing, and learning. With major connectivity investment milestones achieved, particularly with the completion of the Vientiane–Vang Vieng Highway and the Lao PDR–PRC Railway, many new opportunities have opened. It is important to continue upgrading mountain roads as well as district roads within economic corridors to allow for greater ease of matching, sharing, and learning. For budgetary and efficiency reasons, road improvements and their operation and maintenance are needed.

New roads that strengthen connection between cities and economic corridors should be built. For example, an expressway linking Vientiane capital to Viet Nam's Ha Noi would help the Lao PDR to realize it vision of becoming a regional logistics hub. Complementary market infrastructure, such as cold chain storage and modernization of customs clearance services, would help to reduce trade costs. Better-quality road connectivity and improved market infrastructure could substantially increase the market potential of many districts and promote more inclusive growth across the country. After having made major investments in connectivity infrastructure, the Lao PDR will need to ensure enough operation and maintenance of these facilities to ensure that the benefits of these assets are accrued to local communities.

www.ingramcontent.com/pod-product-compliance
Lightning Source LLC
Chambersburg PA
CBHW041246240426
43670CB00028B/3001